A
PREFACE
TO
POLITICS

Titles on Politics in Prometheus's Great Minds Series

Walter Lippmann .... *A Preface to Politics*

See the back of this volume for a complete list of titles in
Prometheus's Great Books in Philosophy and Great Minds series.

A PREFACE TO POLITICS

WALTER LIPPMANN

GREAT MINDS SERIES

 Prometheus Books

59 John Glenn Drive
Amherst, New York 14228-2197

Published 2005 by Prometheus Books

Inquiries should be addressed to
Prometheus Books
59 John Glenn Drive
Amherst, New York 14228–2197

716–691–0133 (x207). FAX: 716–564–2711.
WWW.PROMETHEUSBOOKS.COM

Library of Congress Cataloging-in-Publication Data

Lippmann, Walter, 1889–1974.
    A preface to politics / by Walter Lippmann.
        p. cm.
    Originally published: New York : M. Kennerly, 1913.
    ISBN 1–59102–292–4 (pbk. : alk. paper)
    1. Social problems—United States. 2. United States—Politics and
government. I. Title.

HN64.L55 2005
306.2'0973—dc22

                                                          2005001873

Printed in the United States of America on acid-free paper

Journalist, intellectual, and author, WALTER LIPPMANN accessibly presented his views on contemporary political life, influencing a wide range of figures, such as Jürgen Habermas, Richard Rorty, Cornel West.

The son of German-Jewish parents, Lippmann was born in New York City on September 23, 1889. He attended Harvard University, where he embraced socialism, cofounding the Harvard Socialist Club; edited the *Harvard Monthly*; and served as an assistant to philosopher George Santayana. Lippmann's 1909 graduating class included poet T. S. Eliot and journalist John Reed.

Journalist Lincoln Steffens hired Lippmann as his secretary in 1911. Both supported the Progressive Party's candidate, Theodore Roosevelt, in the 1912 presidential elections. The progressives promised to protect people by enabling the federal government to regulate business. Lippmann's 1913 work, the well-received *A Preface to Politics*, advocated socialist reform. Having little faith in the capability of the masses, Lippmann wanted the government to guide social and economic development. The next year, Lippmann cofounded with Herbert Croly the *New Republic*, a political weekly that offered an alternative to the more mainstream and muck-raking coverage of politics. Lippmann remained associate editor until 1921.

Lippmann's 1914 book *Drift and Mastery* highlighted his turn from socialism. Lippmann aligned with Woodrow Wilson in the presidential elections two years later, supporting in the *New Republic* the democratic candidate and his policy of neutrality in World War I. Persuaded by Col. Edward House, pacifist Lippmann joined Wilson's staff as the assistant to Newton Baker, the secretary of war. With the help of about 125 other researchers, Lippmann drafted an outline for world peace that Wilson used as the basis of his Fourteen Points at the Paris Peace Conference of 1919. Accompanying Wilson to the conference, Lippmann became disappointed with the outcome of the Treaty of Versailles and separated himself from Wilson.

In 1921, Lippmann served as editor of the *New York World* newspaper for two years before moving to the *New York Herald-Tribune*, where he penned his widely syndicated column "Today and Tomorrow." The column earned Lippmann his reputation as a respected political commentator as well as two Pulitzer Prizes—a special one in 1958 and one for international reporting in 1962.

Perhaps Lippmann's most influential book, *Public Opinion* (1922) was inspired by the writings of Sigmund Freud. Unwavering in his distrust of the general public, Lippmann felt that human beings knew too little and based many of their decisions on their illogical impulses. Therefore, Lippmann argued, no model of democracy that inherently trusted the people to govern themselves would succeed. Lippmann's beliefs sparked an ongoing debate with philosopher John Dewey on the average citizen's role in politics and decision-making.

After World War II, Lippmann returned to the more liberal views of his youth. In 1967, he stopped writing his column, in which he had supported seven Democratic and six Republican presidential candidates over thirty years. He opposed both the Korean conflict and the Vietnam War, alienating himself from both political parties. Lippmann died in New York City on December 14, 1974.

Throughout his career, Lippmann wrote articles for more than fifty magazines. His other works include *The Phantom Public* (1925), *A Preface to Morals* (1929), *The Good Society* (1937), *The Cold War* (1947), and *Essays in the Public Philosophy* (1955).

CONTENTS

INTRODUCTION 11

I. Routineer and Inventor 19

II. The Taboo 43

III. The Changing Focus 57

IV. The Golden Rule and After 81

V. Well Meaning But Unmeaning:
The Chicago Vice Report 107

VI. Some Necessary Iconoclasm 135

VII. The Making of Creeds 167

VIII. The Red Herring 199

IX. Revolution and Culture 219

SALE
CASHIER: JOE   06/28/05 15:00

01 DOLE
   500101 16/9994X   1 N   .75
02 SANDWICH
   500501 10541256   3.45
03 NONBOOK/LESSON PL DISCRETE
   400416 10651291
04 LIPPINCOTT/PROFESS DISCRETE
   400418 10652164   1 T   16.00

20.0% Iranian Itap discount
        on Discountable Items   5.72

                   Subtotal   22.37
                        8.80   1.80

    Items   4   Total   24.17

CASH   40.01

              Change Due   15.46

INTRODUCTION

THE most incisive comment on politics to-day is indifference. When men and women begin to feel that elections and legislatures do not matter very much, that politics is a rather distant and unimportant exercise, the reformer might as well put to himself a few searching doubts. Indifference is a criticism that cuts beneath oppositions and wranglings by calling the political method itself into question. Leaders in public affairs recognize this. They know that no attack is so disastrous as silence, that no invective is so blasting as the wise and indulgent smile of the people who do not care. Eager to believe that all the world is as interested as they are, there comes a time when even the reformer is compelled to face the fairly widespread suspicion of the average man that politics is an exhibition in which there is much ado about nothing. But such moments of illumination are rare. They appear in writers who realize how large is the public that doesn't read their books, in reformers who venture to compare the membership list of their league with the census of the United States. Whoever has been granted such a moment of insight knows how exquisitely painful it is. To conquer it men turn generally to their ancient comforter, self-deception: they complain about the stolid, inert masses and the apathy of the people. In a more confidential tone they will tell you that the ordinary citizen is a "hopelessly private person."

A Preface to Politics

The reformer is himself not lacking in stolidity if he can believe such a fiction of a people that crowds about tickers and demands the news of the day before it happens, that trembles on the verge of a panic over the unguarded utterance of a financier, and founds a new religion every month or so. But after a while self-deception ceases to be a comfort. This is when the reformer notices how indifference to politics is settling upon some of the most alert minds of our generation, entering into the attitude of men as capable as any reformer of large and imaginative interests. For among the keenest minds, among artists, scientists and philosophers, there is a remarkable inclination to make a virtue of political indifference. Too passionate an absorption in public affairs is felt to be a somewhat shallow performance, and the reformer is patronized as a well-meaning but rather dull fellow. This is the criticism of men engaged in some genuinely creative labor. Often it is unexpressed, often as not the artist or scientist will join in a political movement. But in the depths of his soul there is, I suspect, some feeling which says to the politician, "Why so hot, my little sir?"

Nothing, too, is more illuminating than the painful way in which many people cultivate a knowledge of public affairs because they have a conscience and wish to do a citizen's duty. Having read a number of articles on the tariff and ploughed through the metaphysics of the currency question, what do they do? They turn with all the more zest to some spontaneous human interest. Perhaps they follow, follow, follow Roosevelt everywhere, and live with him through the emotions of a great battle. But for the affairs of statecraft, for the very policies that a Roosevelt advocates, the interest is largely perfunctory, maintained out of a sense of duty and dropped with a sigh of relief.

That reaction may not be as deplorable as it seems. Pick up your newspaper, read the Congressional Record, run over in your mind the "issues" of a campaign, and then ask yourself whether the average man is entirely to blame because he smiles a bit at Armageddon and refuses to take the politician at his own rhetorical valuation. If men find statecraft uninteresting, may it not be that statecraft *is* uninteresting? I have a more or less professional interest in public affairs; that is to say, I have had opportunity to look at politics from the point of view of the man who is trying to get the attention of people in order to carry through some reform. At first it was a hard confession to make, but the more I saw of politics at first-hand, the more I respected the indifference of the public. There was something monotonously trivial and irrelevant about our reformist enthusiasm, and an appalling justice in that half-conscious criticism which refuses to place politics among the genuine, creative activities of men. Science was valid, art was valid, the poorest grubber in a laboratory was engaged in a real labor, anyone who had found expression in some beautiful object was truly centered. But politics was a personal drama without meaning or a vague abstraction without substance.

Yet there was the fact, just as indisputable as ever, that public affairs do have an enormous and intimate effect upon our lives. They make or unmake us. They are the foundation of that national vigor through which civilizations mature. City and country-side, factories and play, schools and the family are powerful influences in every life, and politics is directly concerned with them. If politics is irrelevant, it is certainly not because its subject matter is unimportant. Public affairs govern our thinking and doing with subtlety and persistence.

The trouble, I figured, must be in the way politics is concerned with the nation's interests. If public business seems to drift aimlessly, its results are, nevertheless, of the highest consequence. In statecraft the penalties and rewards are tremendous. Perhaps the approach is distorted. Perhaps uncriticised assumptions have obscured the real uses of politics. Perhaps an attitude can be worked out which will engage a fresher attention. For there are, I believe, blunders in our political thinking which confuse fictitious activity with genuine achievement, and make it difficult for men to know where they should enlist. Perhaps if we can see politics in a different light, it will rivet our creative interests.

These essays, then, are an attempt to sketch an attitude towards statecraft. I have tried to suggest an approach, to illustrate it concretely, to prepare a point of view. In selecting for the title "A Preface to Politics," I have wished to stamp upon the whole book my own sense that it is a beginning and not a conclusion. I have wished to emphasize that there is nothing in this book which can be drafted into a legislative proposal and presented to the legislature the day after to-morrow. It was not written with the notion that these pages would contain an adequate exposition of modern political method. Much less was it written to further a concrete program. There are, I hope, no assumptions put forward as dogmas.

It is a preliminary sketch for a theory of politics, a

preface to thinking. Like all speculation about human affairs, it is the result of a grapple with problems as they appear in the experience of one man. For though a personal vision may at times assume an eloquent and universal language, it is well never to forget that all philosophies are the language of particular men.

W. L.

46 East 80th Street, NEW YORK CITY, January 1913.

A
PREFACE
TO
POLITICS

CHAPTER I

ROUTINEER AND INVENTOR

POLITICS does not exist for the sake of demonstrating the superior righteousness of anybody. It is not a competition in deportment. In fact, before you can begin to think about politics at all you have to abandon the notion that there is a war between good men and bad men. That is one of the great American superstitions. More than any other fetish it has ruined our sense of political values by glorifying the pharisee with his vain cruelty to individuals and his unfounded approval of himself. You have only to look at the Senate of the United States, to see how that body is capable of turning itself into a court of preliminary hearings for the Last Judgment, wasting its time and our time and absorbing public enthusiasm and newspaper scareheads. For a hundred needs of the nation it has no thought, but about the precise morality of an historical transaction eight years old there is a meticulous interest. Whether in the Presidential Campaign of 1904 Roosevelt was aware that the ancient tradition of corporate subscriptions had or had not been followed, and the exact and ultimate measure of the guilt that knowledge would have implied—this in the year 1912 is enough to start the Senate on a protracted man-hunt.

Now if one half of the people is bent upon proving how wicked a man is and the other half is determined to show how good he is, neither half will think very much about the nation. An innocent paragraph in the New York Evening Post for August 27, 1912, gives the whole performance away. It shows as clearly as words could how disastrous the good-and-bad-man theory is to political thinking:

> Provided the first hearing takes place on September 30, it is expected that the developments will be made with a view to keeping the Colonel on the defensive. After the beginning of October, it is pointed out, the evidence before the Committee should keep him so busy explaining and denying that the country will not hear much Bull Moose doctrine.

Whether you like the Roosevelt doctrines or not, there can be no two opinions about such an abuse of morality. It is a flat public loss, another attempt to befuddle our thinking. For if politics is merely a guerilla war between the bribed and the unbribed, then statecraft is not a human service but a moral testing ground. It is a public amusement, a melodrama of real life, in which a few conspicuous characters are tried, and it resembles nothing so much as schoolboy hazing which we are told exists for the high purpose of detecting a "yellow streak." But even though we desired it there would be no way of establishing any clear-cut difference in politics between the angels and the imps. The angels are largely self-appointed, being somewhat more sensitive to other people's tar than their own.

But if the issue is not between honesty and dishonesty, where is it?

If you stare at a checkerboard you can see it as black on red, or red on black, as series of horizontal, vertical or diagonal steps which recede or protrude. The longer you look the more patterns you can trace, and the more certain it becomes that there is no single way of looking at the board. So with political issues. There is no obvious cleavage which everyone recognizes. Many patterns appear in the national life. The "progressives" say the issue is between "Privilege" and the "People"; the Socialists, that it is between the "working class" and the "master class." An apologist for dynamite told me once that society was divided into the weak and the strong, and there are people who draw a line between Philistia and Bohemia.

When you rise up and announce that the conflict is between this and that, you mean that this particular conflict interests you. The issue of good-and-bad-men interests this nation to the exclusion of almost all others. But experience shows, I believe, that it is a fruitless conflict and a wasting enthusiasm. Yet some distinction must be drawn if we are to act at all in politics. With nothing we are for and nothing to oppose, we are merely neutral. This cleavage in public affairs is the most important choice we are called upon to make. In large measure it determines the rest of our thinking. Now some issues are fertile; some are not. Some lead to spacious results; others are blind alleys. With this in mind I wish to suggest that the distinction most worth emphasizing to-day is between those who regard government as a routine to be administered and those who regard it as a problem to be solved.

The class of routineers is larger than the conservatives. The man who will follow precedent, but never create one, is merely an obvious example of the routineer. You find him desperately numerous in the civil service, in the official bureaus. To him government is something given as unconditionally, as absolutely as ocean or hill. He goes on winding the tape that he finds. His imagination has rarely extricated itself from under the administrative machine to gain any sense of what a human, temporary contraption the whole affair is. What he thinks is the heavens above him is nothing but the roof.

He is the slave of routine. He can boast of somewhat more spiritual cousins in the men who reverence their ancestors' independence, who feel, as it were, that a disreputable great-grandfather is necessary to a family's respectability. These are the routineers gifted with historical sense. They take their forefathers with enormous solemnity. But one mistake is rarely avoided: they imitate the old-fashioned thing their grandfather did, and ignore the originality which enabled him to do it.

If tradition were a reverent record of those crucial moments when men burst through their habits, a love of the past would not be the butt on which every sophomoric radical can practice his wit. But almost always tradition is nothing but a record and a machine-made imitation of the habits that our ancestors created. The average conservative is a slave to the most incidental and trivial part of his forefathers' glory—to the archaic formula which happened to express their genius or the eighteenth century contrivance by which for a time it was served. To reverence Washington they wear a powdered wig; they do honor to Lincoln by cultivating awkward hands and ungainly feet.

It is fascinating to watch this kind of conservative in action. From Senator Lodge, for example, we do not expect any new perception of popular need. We know that probably his deepest sincerity is an attempt to reproduce the atmosphere of the Senate a hundred years ago. The manners of Mr. Lodge have that immobility which comes from too much gazing at bad statues of dead statesmen.

Yet just because a man is in opposition to Senator Lodge there is no guarantee that he has freed himself from the routineer's habit of mind. A prejudice against some mannerism or a dislike of pretensions may merely cloak some other kind of routine. Take the "good government" attitude. No fresh insight is behind that. It does not promise anything; it does not offer to contribute new values to human life. The machine which exists is accepted in all its essentials: the "goo-goo" yearns for a somewhat smoother rotation.

Often as not the very effort to make the existing machine run more perfectly merely makes matters worse. For the tinkering reformer is frequently one of the worst of the routineers. Even machines are not altogether inflexible, and sometimes what the reformer regards as a sad deviation from the original plans is a poor rickety attempt to adapt the machine to changing conditions. Think what would have happened had we actually remained stolidly faithful to every intention of the Fathers. Think what would happen if every statute were enforced. By the sheer force of circumstances we have twisted constitutions and laws to some approximation of our needs. A changing country has managed to live in spite of a static government machine. Perhaps Bernard Shaw was right when he said that "the famous Constitution survives only because whenever any corner of it gets into the way of the accumulating dollar it is pettishly knocked off and thrown away. Every social development, however beneficial and inevitable from the public point of view, is met, not by an intelligent adaptation of the social structure to its novelties but by a panic and a cry of Go Back."

I am tempted to go further and put into the same class all those radicals who wish simply to substitute some other kind of machine for the one we have. Though not all of them would accept the name, these reformers are simply utopia-makers in action. Their perceptions are more critical than the ordinary conservatives'. They do see that humanity is badly squeezed in the existing mould. They have enough imagination to conceive a different one. But they have an infinite faith in moulds. This routine they don't believe in, but they believe in their own: if you could put the country under a new "system," then human affairs would run automatically for the welfare of all. Some improvement there might be, but as almost all men are held in an iron devotion to their own creations, the routine reformers are simply working for another conservatism, and not for any continuing liberation.

The type of statesman we must oppose to the routineer is one who regards all social organization as an instrument. Systems, institutions and mechanical contrivances have for him no virtue of their own: they are valuable only when they serve the purposes of men. He uses them, of course, but with a constant sense that men have made them, that new ones can be devised, that only an effort of the will can keep machinery in its place. He has no faith whatever in automatic governments. While the routineers see machinery and precedents revolving with mankind as puppets, he puts the deliberate, conscious, willing individual at the center of his philosophy. This reversal is pregnant with a new outlook for statecraft. I hope to show that it alone can keep step with life; it alone is humanly relevant; and it alone achieves valuable results.

Call this man a political creator or a political inventor. The essential quality of him is that he makes that part of existence which has experience the master of it. He serves the ideals of human feelings, not the tendencies of mechanical things.

The difference between a phonograph and the human voice is that the phonograph must sing the song which is stamped upon it. Now there are days—I suspect the vast majority of them in most of our lives—when we grind out the thing that is stamped upon us. It may be the governing of a city, or teaching school, or running a business. We do not get out of bed in the morning because we are eager for the day; something external—we often call it our duty—throws off the bed-clothes, complains that the shaving water isn't hot, puts us into the subway and lands us at our office in season for punching the time-check. We revolve with the business for three or four hours, signing letters, answering telephones, checking up lists, and perhaps towards twelve o'clock the prospect of lunch puts a touch of romance upon life. Then because our days are so unutterably the same, we turn to the newspapers, we go to the magazines and read only the "stuff with punch," we seek out a "show" and drive serious playwrights into the poorhouse. "You can go through contemporary life," writes Wells, "fudging and evading, indulging and slacking, never really hungry nor frightened nor passionately stirred, your highest moment a mere senti-mental orgasm, and your first real contact with primary and elementary necessities the sweat of your death-bed."

The world grinds on: we are a fly on the wheel. That sense of an impersonal machine going on with endless reit-eration is an experience that imaginative politicians face. Often as not they disguise it under heroic phrases and still louder affirmation, just as most of us hide our cowardly submission to monotony under some word like duty, loy-alty, conscience. If you have ever been an office-holder or been close to officials, you must surely have been appalled by the grim way in which committee-meetings, verbose reports, flamboyant speeches, requests, and delegations hold the statesman in a mind-destroying grasp. Perhaps this is the reason why it has been necessary to retire Theodore Roosevelt from public life every now and then in order to give him a chance to learn something new. Every statesman like every professor should have his sabbatical year.

The revolt against the service of our own mechanical habits is well known to anyone who has followed modern thought. As a sharp example one might point to Thomas Davidson, whom William James called "individualist á out-rance" . . . "Reprehending (mildly) a certain chapter of my own on 'Habit,' he said that it was a fixed rule with him to form no regular habits. When he found himself in danger of settling into even a good one, he made a point of interrupting it."

Such men are the sparkling streams that flow through the dusty stretches of a nation. They invigorate and emphasize those times in your own life when each day is new. Then you are alive, then you drive the world before you. The business, however difficult, shapes itself to your effort; you seem to manage detail with an inferior part of yourself, while the real soul of you is active, planning, light. "I wanted thought like an edge of steel and desire like a flame." Eager with sympathy, you and your work are reflected from many angles. You have become luminous.

Some people are predominantly eager and wilful. The world does not huddle and bend them to a task. They are not, as we say, creatures of environment, but creators of it. Of other people's environment they become the most active part—the part which sets the fashion. What they initiate, others imitate. Theirs is a kind of intrinsic prestige. These are the natural leaders of men, whether it be as head of the gang or as founder of a religion.

It is, I believe, this power of being aggressively active towards the world which gives man a miraculous assurance that the world is something he can make. In creative moments men always draw upon "some secret spring of certainty, some fundamental well into which no disturbing glimmers penetrate." But this is no slack philosophy, for the chance is denied by which we can lie back upon the perfection of some mechanical contrivance. Yet in the light of it government becomes alert to a process of continual creation, an unceasing invention of forms to meet constantly changing needs.

This philosophy is not only difficult to practice: it is elusive when you come to state it. For our political language was made to express a routine conception of government. It comes to us from the Eighteenth Century. And no matter how much we talk about the infusion of the "evolutionary" point of view into all of modern thought, when the test is made political practice shows itself almost virgin to the idea. Our theories assume, and our language is fitted to thinking of government as a frame—Massachusetts, I believe, actually calls her fundamental law the Frame of Government. We picture political institutions as mechanically constructed contrivances within which the nation's life is contained and compelled to approximate some abstract idea of justice or liberty. These frames have very little elasticity, and we take it as an historical commonplace that sooner or later a revolution must come to burst the frame apart. Then a new one is constructed.

Our own Federal Constitution is a striking example of this machine conception of government. It is probably the most important instance we have of the deliberate application of a mechanical philosophy to human affairs. Leaving out all question of the Fathers' ideals, looking simply at the bias which directed their thinking, is there in all the world a more plain-spoken attempt to contrive an automatic governor—a machine which would preserve its balance without the need of taking human nature into account? What other explanation is there for the naïve faith of the Fathers in the "symmetry" of executive, legislature, and judiciary; in the fantastic attempts to circumvent human folly by balancing it with vetoes and checks? No insight into the evident fact that power upsets all mechanical foresight and gravitates

[*28*]

toward the natural leaders seems to have illuminated those historic deliberations. The Fathers had a rather pale god, they had only a speaking acquaintance with humanity, so they put their faith in a scaffold, and it has been part of our national piety to pretend that they succeeded.

They worked with the philosophy of their age. Living in the Eighteenth Century, they thought in the images of Newton and Montesquieu. "The Government of the United States," writes Woodrow Wilson, "was constructed upon the Whig theory of political dynamics, which was a sort of unconscious copy of the Newtonian theory of the universe. ... As Montesquieu pointed out to them (the English Whigs) in his lucid way, they had sought to balance executive, legislative and judiciary off against one another by a series of checks and counterpoises, which Newton might readily have recognized as suggestive of the mechanism of the heavens." No doubt this automatic and balanced theory of government suited admirably that distrust of the people which seems to have been a dominant feeling among the Fathers. For they were the conservatives of their day: between '76 and '89 they had gone the usual way of opportunist radicals. But had they written the Constitution in the fire of their youth, they might have made it more democratic,—I doubt whether they would have made it less mechanical. The rebellious spirit of Tom Paine expressed itself in logical formulae as inflexible to the pace of life as did the more contented Hamilton's. This is a determinant which burrows beneath our ordinary classification of progressive and reactionary to the spiritual habits of a period.

If you look into the early utopias of Fourier and Saint-

Simon, or better still into the early trade unions, this same faith that a government can be made to work mechanically is predominant everywhere. All the devices of rotation in office, short terms, undelegated authority are simply attempts to defeat the half-perceived fact that power will not long stay diffused. It is characteristic of these primitive democracies that they worship Man and distrust men. They cling to some arrangement, hoping against experience that a government freed from human nature will automatically produce human benefits. To-day within the Socialist Party there is perhaps the greatest surviving example of the desire to offset natural leadership by artificial contrivance. It is an article of faith among orthodox socialists that personalities do not count, and I sincerely believe I am not exaggerating the case when I say that their ideal of government is like Gordon Craig's ideal of the theater—the acting is to be done by a row of supermarionettes. There is a myth among socialists to which all are expected to subscribe, that initiative springs anonymously out of the mass of the people,—that there are no "leaders," that the conspicuous figures are no more influential than the figurehead on the prow of a ship.

This is one of the paradoxes of the democratic movement—that it loves a crowd and fears the individuals who compose it—that the religion of humanity should have had no faith in human beings. Jealous of all individuals, democracies have turned to machines. They have tried to blot out human prestige, to minimize the influence of personality. That there is historical justification for this fear is plain enough. To put it briefly, democracy is afraid of the tyrant. That explains, but does not justify. Governments have to be carried on by men, however much we distrust them. Nobody has yet invented a mechanically beneficent sovereign.

Democracy has put an unfounded faith in automatic contrivances. Because it left personality out of its speculation, it rested in the empty faith that it had excluded it from reality. But in the actual stress of life these frictions do not survive ten minutes. Public officials do not become political marionettes, though people pretend that they are. When theory runs against the grain of living forces, the result is a deceptive theory of politics. If the real government of the United States "had, in fact," as Woodrow Wilson says, "been a machine governed by mechanically automatic balances, it would have had no history; but it was not, and its history has been rich with the influence and personalities of the men who have conducted it and made it a living reality." Only by violating the very spirit of the constitution have we been able to preserve the letter of it. For behind that balanced plan there grew up what Senator Beveridge has called so brilliantly the "invisible government," an empire of natural groups about natural leaders. Parties are such groups: they have had a power out of all proportion to the intentions of the Fathers. Behind the parties has grown up the "political machine"—falsely called a machine, the very opposite of one in fact, a natural sovereignty, I believe. The really rigid and mechanical thing is the charter behind which Tammany works. For Tammany is the real government that has defeated a mechanical foresight. Tammany is not a freak, a strange and monstrous excrescence. Its structure and the laws of its life are, I believe, typical of all real sovereignties. You can find Tammany duplicated wherever there is a social group to be governed—in trade unions, in clubs, in boys' gangs, in the Four Hundred, in the Socialist Party. It is an accretion of power around a center of influence, cemented by patronage, graft, favors, friendship, loyalties, habits,—a human grouping, a natural pyramid.

Only recently have we begun tot see that the "political ring" is not something confined to public life. It was Lincoln Steffens, I believe, who first perceived that fact. For a time it was my privilege to work under him on an investigation of the "Money Power." The leading idea was different from customary "muckraking." We were looking not for the evils of Big Business, but for its anatomy. Mr. Steffens came to the subject with a first-hand knowledge of politics. He knew the "invisible government" of cities, states, and the nation. He knew how the boss worked, how he organized his power. When Mr. Steffens approached the vast confusion and complication of big business, he needed some hypothesis to guide him through that maze of facts. He made a bold and brilliant guess, an hypothesis. To govern a life insurance company, Mr. Steffens argued, was just as much "government" as to run a city. What if political methods existed in the realm of business? The investigation was never carried through completely, but we did study the methods by which several life and fire insurance companies, banks, two or three railroads, and several industrials are controlled. We found that the anatomy of Big Business was strikingly like that of Tammany Hall: the same pyramiding of influence, the same tendency of power to center on individuals who did not necessarily sit in the official seats, the same effort of human organization to grow independently of legal arrangements. Thus in the life insurance companies, and the Hughes investigation supports this, the real power was held not by the president, not by the voters or policyholders, but by men who were not even directors. After a while we took it as a matter of course that the head of a company was an administrative dummy, with a dependence on unofficial power similar to that of Governor Dix on Boss Murphy. That seems to be typical of the whole economic life of this country. It is controlled by groups of men whose influence extends like a web to smaller, tributary groups, cutting across all official boundaries and designations, making short work of all legal formulæ, and exercising sovereignty regardless of the little fences we erect to keep it in bounds.

A glimpse into the labor world revealed very much the same condition. The boss, and the bosslet, the heeler—the men who are "it"—all are there exercising the real power, the power that independently of charters and elections decides what shall happen. I don't wish to have this regarded as necessarily malign. It seems so now because we put our faith in the ideal arrangements which it disturbs. But if we could come to face it squarely—to see that that is what sovereignty is—that if we are to use human power for human purposes we must turn to the realities of it, then we shall have gone far towards leaving behind us the futile hopes of mechanical perfection so consantly blasted by natural facts.

The invisible government is malign. But the evil doesn't come from the fact that it plays horse with the Newtonian theory of the constitution. What is dangerous about it is that we do not see it, cannot use it, and are compelled to submit to it. The nature of political power we shall not change. If that is the way human societies organize sovereignty, the sooner we face that fact the better. For the object of democracy is not to imitate the rhythm of the stars but to harness political power to the nation's need. If corporations and governments have indeed gone on a joy ride the business of reform is not to set up fences, Sherman Acts and injunctions into which they can bump, but to take the wheel and to steer.

The corruption of which we hear so much is certainly not accounted for when you have called it dishonesty. It is too widespread for any such glib explanation. When you see how business controls politics, it certainly is not very illuminating to call the successful business men of a nation criminals. Yet I suppose that all of them violate the law. May not this constant dodging or hurdling of statutes be a sign that there is something the matter with the statutes? Is it not possible that graft is the cracking and bursting of the receptacles in which we have tried to constrain the business of this country? It seems possible that business has had to control politics because its laws were so stupidly obstructive. In the trust agitation this is especially plausible. For there is every reason to believe that concentration is a world-wide tendency, made possible at first by mechanical inventions, fostered by the disastrous experiences of competition, and accepted by business men through contagion and imitation. Certainly the trusts increase. Wherever politics is rigid and hostile to that tendency, there is irritation and struggle, but the agglomeration goes on. Hindered by political conditions, the process becomes secretive and morbid. The trust is not checked, but it is perverted. In 1910

the "American Banker" estimated that there were 1,198 corporations with 8,110 subsidiaries liable to all the penalties
of the Sherman Act. Now this concentration must represent
a profound impetus in the business world—an impetus
which certainly cannot be obliterated, even if anyone were
foolish enough to wish it. I venture to suggest that much of
what is called "corruption" is the odor of a decaying political system done to death by an economic growth.

It is our desperate adherence to an old method that has
produced the confusion of political life. Because we have
insisted upon looking at government as a frame and governing as a routine, because in short we have been static in
our theories, politics has such an unreal relation to actual
conditions. Feckless—that is what our politics is. It is literally eccentric: it has been centered mechanically instead of
vitally. We have, it seems, been seduced by a fictitious
analogy: we have hoped for machine regularity when we
needed human initiative and leadership, when life was
crying that its inventive abilities should be freed.

Roosevelt in his term did much to center government
truly. For a time natural leadership and nominal position
coincided, and the administration became in a measure a
real sovereignty. The routine conception dwindled, and the
Roosevelt appointees went at issues as problems to be
solved. They may have been mistaken: Roosevelt may be
uncritical in his judgments. But the fact remains that the
Roosevelt régime gave a new prestige to the Presidency by
effecting through it the greatest release of political invention in a generation. Contrast it with the Taft administration,
and the quality is set in relief. Taft was the perfect routineer

trying to run government as automatically as possible. His sincerity consisted in utter respect for form: he denied himself whatever leadership he was capable of, and outwardly at least he tried to "balance" the government. His greatest passions seem to be purely administrative and legal. The people did not like it. They said it was dead. They were right. They had grown accustomed to a humanly liberating atmosphere in which formality was an instrument instead of an idol. They had seen the Roosevelt influence adding to the resources of life—irrigation, and waterways, conservation, the Panama Canal, the "country life" movement. They knew these things were achieved through initiative that burst through formal restrictions, and they applauded wildly. It was only a taste, but it was a taste, a taste of what government might be like.

The opposition was instructive. Apart from those who feared Roosevelt for selfish reasons, his enemies were men who loved an orderly adherence to traditional methods. They shivered in the emotional gale; they obstructed and the gale became destructive. They felt that, along with obviously good things, this sudden national fertility might breed a monster—that a leadership like Roosevelt's might indeed prove dangerous, as giving birth may lead to death.

What the methodically-minded do not see is that the sterility of a routine is far more appalling. Not everyone may feel that to push out into the untried, and take risks for big prizes, is worth while. Men will tell you that government has no business to undertake an adventure, to make experiments. They think that safety lies in repetition, that if you do nothing, nothing will be done to you. It's a mistake due to poverty of imagination and inability to learn from experience. Even the timidest soul dare not "stand pat." The indictment against mere routine in government is a staggering one.

For while statesmen are pottering along doing the same thing year in, year out, putting up the tariff one year and down the next, passing appropriation bills and recodifying laws, the real forces in the country do not stand still. Vast changes, economic and psychological, take place, and these changes demand new guidance. But the routineers are always unprepared. It has become one of the grim trade jokes of innovators that the one thing you can count upon is that the rulers will come to think that they are the apex of human development. For a queer effect of responsibility on men is that it makes them try to be as much like machines as possible. Tammany itself becomes rigid when it is too successful, and only defeat seems to give it new life. Success makes men rigid and they tend to exalt stability over all the other virtues; tired of the effort of willing they become fanatics about conservatism. But conditions change whether statesmen wish them to or not; society must have new institutions to fit new wants, and all that rigid conservatism can do is to make the transitions difficult. Violent revolutions may be charged up to the unreadiness of statesmen. It is because they will not see, or cannot see, that feudalism is dead, that chattel slavery is antiquated; it is because they have not the wisdom and the audacity to anticipate these great social changes; it is because they insist upon standing pat that we have French Revolutions and Civil Wars.

But statesmen who had decided that at last men were to

be the masters of their own history, instead of its victims, would face politics in a truly revolutionary manner. It would give a new outlook to statesmanship, turning it from the mere preservation of order, the administration of political machinery and the guarding of ancient privilege to the invention of new political forms, the prevision of social wants, and the preparation for new economic growths.

Such a statesmanship would in the '80's have prepared for the trust movement. There would have been nothing miraculous in such foresight. Standard Oil was dominant by the beginning of the '80's, and concentration had begun in sugar, steel and other basic industries. Here was an economic tendency of revolutionary significance—the organization of business in a way that was bound to change the outlook of a whole nation. It had vast potentialities for good and evil—all it wanted was harnessing and directing. But the new thing did not fit into the little outlines and verbosities which served as a philosophy for our political hacks. So they gaped at it and let it run wild, called it names, and threw stones at it. And by that time the force was too big for them. An alert statesmanship would have facilitated the process of concentration; would have made provision for those who were cast aside; would have been an ally of trust building, and by that very fact it would have had an internal grip on the trust—it would have kept the trust's inner workings public; it could have bent the trust to social uses.

This is not mere wisdom after the event. In the '80's there were hundreds of thousands of people in the world who understood that the trust was a natural economic growth. Karl Marx had proclaimed it some thirty years before, and it was a widely circulated idea. Is it asking too much of a statesman if we expect him to know political theory and to balance it with the facts he sees? By the '90's surely, the egregious folly of a Sherman Anti-Trust Law should have been evident to any man who pretended to political leadership. Yet here it is the year 1912 and that monument of economic ignorance and superstition is still worshiped with the lips by two out of the three big national parties.

Another movement—like that of the trust—is gathering strength to-day. It is the unification of wage-workers. We stand in relation to it as the men of the '80's did to the trusts. It is the complement of that problem. It also has vast potentialities for good and evil. It, too, demands understanding and direction. It, too, will not be stopped by hard names or injunctions.

What we loosely call "syndicalism" is a tendency that no statesman can overlook to-day without earning the jeers of his children. This labor movement has a destructive and constructive energy within it. On its beneficent side it promises a new professional interest in work, self-education, and the co-operative management of industry. But this creative power is constantly choked off because the unions are compelled to fight for their lives—the more opposition they meet the more you are likely to see of sabotage, direct action, the grève perlée—the less chance there is for the educative forces to show themselves. Then, the more violent syndicalism proves itself to be, the more hysterically we bait it in the usual vicious circle of ignorance.

But who amongst us is optimistic enough to hope that the men who sit in the mighty positions are going to make a better show of themselves than their predecessors did over the trust problem? It strains hope a little too much. Those men in Washington, most of them lawyers, are so educated that they are practically incapable of meeting a new condition. All their training plus all their natural ossification of mind is hostile to invention. You cannot endow even the best machine with initiative; the jolliest steam-roller will not plant flowers.

The thought-processes in Washington are too lumbering for the needs of this nation. Against that evil muckraking ought to be directed. Those senators and representatives are largely irrelevant; they are not concerned with realities. Their dishonesties are comparatively insignificant. The scorn of the public should be turned upon the emptiness of political thought, upon the fact that those men seem without even a conception of the nation's needs. And while they maunder along they stifle the forces of life which are trying to break through. It was nothing but the insolence of the routineer that forced Gifford Pinchot out of the Forest Service. Pinchot in respect to his subject was a fine political inventor. But routine forced him out—into what?—into the moil and toil of fighting for offices, and there he has cut a poor figure indeed. You may say that he has had to spend his energy trying to find a chance to use his power. What a wanton waste of talent is that for a civilized nation! Wiley is another case of the creative mind harassed by the routineers. Judge Lindsey is another—a fine, constructive children's judge compelled to be a politician. And of our misuse of the Rockefellers and Carnegies—the retrospect is appalling. Here was industrial genius unquestionably beyond the ordinary. What did this nation do with it? It found no public use for talent. It left that to operate in darkness—then opinion rose in an empty fury, made an outlaw of one and a platitudinous philanthropist of the other. It could lynch one as a moral monster, when as a matter of fact his ideals were commonplace; it could proclaim one a great benefactor when in truth he was a rather dull old gentleman. Abused out of all reason or praised irrelevantly—the one thing this nation has not been able to do with these men is to use their genius. It is this life-sapping quality of our politics that should be fought—its wanton waste of the initiatives we have—its stupid indifference.

We need a new sense of political values. These times require a different order of thinking. We cannot expect to meet our problems with a few inherited ideas, uncriticised assumptions, a foggy vocabulary, and a machine philosophy. Our political thinking needs the infusion of contemporary insights. The enormous vitality that is regenerating other interests can be brought into the service of politics. Our primary care must be to keep the habits of the mind flexible and adapted to the movement of real life. The only way to control our destiny is to work with it. In politics, at least, we stoop to conquer. There is no use, no heroism, in butting against the inevitable, yet nothing is entirely inevitable. There is always some choice, some opportunity for human direction.

It is not easy. It is far easier to treat life as if it were dead, men as if they were dolls. It is everlastingly difficult to keep the mind flexible and alert. The rule of thumb is not here. To follow the pace of living requires enormous vigilance and sympathy. No one can write conclusively about it. Compared with this creative statesmanship, the administering of a routine or the battle for a platitude is a very simple affair. But genuine politics is not an inhuman task. Part of the genuineness is its unpretentious humanity. I am not creating the figure of an ideal statesman out of some inner fancy. That is just the deepest error of our political thinking—to talk of politics without reference to human beings. The creative men appear in public life in spite of the cold blanket the politicians throw over them. Really statesmanlike things are done, inventions are made. But this real achievement comes to us confused, mixed with much that is contradictory. Political inventors are to-day largely unconscious of their purpose, and, so, defenceless against the distraction of their routineer enemies.

Lacking a philosophy they are defenceless against their own inner tendency to sink into repetition. As a witty Frenchman remarked, many geniuses become their own disciples. This is true when the attention is slack, and effort has lost its direction. We have elaborate governmental mechanisms—like the tariff, for example, which we go on making more "scientific" year in, year out—having long since lost sight of their human purpose. They may be defeating the very ends they were meant to serve. We cling to constitutions out of "loyalty." We trudge in the treadmill and call it love of our ancient institutions. We emulate the mule, that greatest of all routineers.

CHAPTER II

THE TABOO

OUR government has certainly not measured up to expectations. Even chronic admirers of the "balance" and "symmetry" of the Constitution admit either by word or deed that it did not foresee the whole history of the American people. Poor bewildered statesmen, unused to any notion of change, have seen the national life grow to a monstrous confusion and sprout monstrous evils by the way. Men and women clamored for remedies, vowed, shouted and insisted that their "official servants" do something—something statesmanlike—to abate so much evident wrong. But their representatives had very little more than a frock coat and a slogan as equipment for the task. Trained to interpret a constitution instead of life, these statesmen faced with historic helplessness the vociferations of ministers, muckrakers, labor leaders, women's clubs, granges and reformers' leagues. Out of a tumultuous medley appeared the common theme of public opinion—that the leaders should lead, that the governors should govern.

The trusts had appeared, labor was restless, vice seemed to be corrupting the vitality of the nation. Statesmen had to do something. Their training was legal and therefore utterly inadequate, but it was all they had. They became panicky and reverted to an ancient superstition. They forbade the existence of evil by law. They made it anathema. They pronounced it damnable. They threatened to club it. They issued a legislative curse, and called upon the district attorney to do the rest. They started out to abolish human instincts, check economic tendencies and repress social changes by laws prohibiting them. They turned to this sanctified ignorance which is rampant in almost any nursery, which presides at family councils, flourishes among "reformers"; which from time immemorial has haunted legislatures and courts. Under the spell of it men try to stop drunkenness by closing the saloons; when poolrooms shock them they call a policeman; if Haywood becomes annoying, they procure an injunction. They meet the evils of dance halls by barricading them; they go forth to battle against vice by raiding brothels and fining prostitutes. For trusts there is a Sherman Act. In spite of all experience they cling desperately to these superstitions.

It is the method of the taboo, as naïve as barbarism, as ancient as human failure.

There is a law against suicide. It is illegal for a man to kill himself. What it means in practice, of course, is that there is punishment waiting for a man who doesn't succeed in killing himself. We say to the man who is tired of life that if he bungles we propose to make this world still less attractive by clapping him into jail. I know an economist who has a scheme for keeping down the population by refusing very poor people a marriage license. He used to teach Sunday school and deplore promiscuity. In the annual report of the president of a distilling company I once saw the statement that business had increased in the "dry" states. In a prohibition town where I lived you could drink all you wanted by belonging to a "club" or winking at the druggist. And in another city where Sunday closing was strictly enforced, a minister told me with painful surprise that the Monday police blotter showed less drunks and more wife-beaters.

We pass a law against race-track gambling and add to the profits from faro. We raid the faro joints, and drive gambling into the home, where poker and bridge whist are taught to children who follow their parents' example. We deprive anarchists of free speech by the heavy hand of a police magistrate, and furnish them with a practical instead of a theoretical argument against government. We answer strikes with bayonets, and make treason one of the rights of man.

Everybody knows that when you close the dance halls you fill the parks. Men who in their youth took part in "crusades" against the Tenderloin now admit in a crestfallen way that they succeeded merely in sprinkling the Tenderloin through the whole city. Over twenty years ago we formulated a sweeping taboo against trusts. Those same twenty years mark the centralization of industry.

The routineer in a panic turns to the taboo. Whatever does not fit into his rigid little scheme of things must have its head chopped off. Now human nature and the changing social forces it generates are the very material which fit least well into most little schemes of things. A man cannot sleep in his cradle: whatever is useful must in the nature of life become useless. We employ our instruments and abandon them. But nothing so simply true as that prevails in politics. When a government routine conflicts with the nation's purposes—the statesman actually makes a virtue of his loyalty to the routine. His practice is to ignore human character and pay no attention to social forces. The shallow presumption is that undomesticated impulses can be obliterated; that world-wide economic inventions can be stamped out by jailing millionaires—and acting in the spirit of Mr. Chesterton's man Fipps "who went mad and ran about the country with an axe, hacking branches off the trees whenever there were not the same number on both sides." The routineer is, of course, the first to decry every radical proposal as "against human nature." But the stand-pat mind has forfeited all right to speak for human nature. It has devoted the centuries to torturing men's instincts, stamping on them, passing laws against them, lifting its eyebrows at the thought of them—doing everything but trying to understand them. The same people who with daily insistence say that innovators ignore facts are in the absurd predicament of trying to still human wants with petty taboos. Social systems like ours, which do not even feed and house men and women, which deny pleasure, cramp play, ban adventure, propose celibacy and grind out monotony, are a clear confession of sterility in statesmanship. And politics, however pretentiously rhetorical about ideals, is irrelevant if the only method it knows is to ostracize the desires it cannot manage.

Suppose that statesmen transferred their reverence from the precedents and mistakes of their ancestors to the human material which they have set out to govern. Suppose they looked mankind in the face and asked themselves what was the result of answering evil with a prohibition. Such an exercise would, I fear, involve a considerable strain on what reformers call their moral sensibilities. For human nature is a rather shocking affair if you come to it with ordinary romantic optimism. Certainly the human nature that figures in most political thinking is a wraith that never was—not even in the souls of politicians. "Idealism" creates an abstraction and then shudders at a reality which does not answer to it. Now statesmen who have set out to deal with actual life must deal with actual people. They cannot afford an inclusive pessimism about mankind. Let them have the consistency and good sense to cease bothering about men if men's desires seem intrinsically evil. Moral judgment about the ultimate quality of character is dangerous to a politician. He is too constantly tempted to call a policeman when he disapproves.

We must study our failures. Gambling and drink, for example, produce much misery. But what reformers have to learn is that men don't gamble just for the sake of violating the law. They do so because something within them is satisfied by betting or drinking. To erect a ban doesn't stop the want. It merely prevents its satisfaction. And since this desire for stimulants or taking a chance at a prize is older and far more deeply rooted in the nature of men than love of the Prohibition Party or reverence for laws made at Albany, people will contrive to drink and gamble in spite of the acts of a legislature.

A man may take liquor for a variety of reasons: he may be thirsty; or depressed; or unusually happy; he may want the companionship of a saloon, or he may hope to forget a scolding wife. Perhaps he needs a "bracer" in a weary hunt for a job. Perhaps he has a terrible craving for alcohol. He does not take a drink so that he may become an habitual drunkard, or be locked up in jail, or get into a brawl, or lose his job, or go insane. These are what he might call the unfortunate by-products of his desire. If once he could find something which would do for him what liquor does, without hurting him as liquor does, there would be no problem of drink. Bernard Shaw says he has found that substitute in going to church when there's no service. Goethe wrote "The Sorrows of Werther" in order to get rid of his own. Many an unhappy lover has found peace by expressing his misery in sonnet form. The problem is to find something for the common man who is not interested in contemporary churches and who can't write sonnets.

When the socialists in Milwaukee began to experiment with municipal dances they were greeted with indignant protests from the "anti-vice" element and with amused contempt by the newspaper paragraphers. The dances were discontinued, and so the belief in their failure is complete. I think, though, that Mayor Seidel's defense would by itself make this experiment memorable. He admitted freely the worst that can be said against the ordinary dance hall. So far he was with the petty reformers. Then he pointed out with considerable vehemence that dance halls were an urgent social necessity. At that point he had transcended the mind of the petty reformer completely. "We propose," said Seidel, "to go into competition with the devil."

Nothing deeper has come from an American mayor in a long, long time. It is the point that Jane Addams makes in the opening pages of that wisely sweet book, "The Spirit of

Youth and the City Streets." She calls attention to the fact that the modern state has failed to provide for pleasure. "This stupid experiment," she writes, "of organizing work and failing to organize play has, of course, brought about a fine revenge. The love of pleasure will not be denied, and when it has turned into all sorts of malignant and vicious appetites, then we, the middle-aged, grow quite distracted and resort to all sorts of restrictive measures."

For human nature seems to have wants that must be filled. If nobody else supplies them, the devil will. The demand for pleasure, adventure, romance has been left to the devil's catering for so long a time that most people think he inspires the demand. He doesn't. Our neglect is the devil's opportunity. What we should use, we let him abuse, and the corruption of the best things, as Hume remarked, produces the worst. Pleasure in our cities has become tied to lobster palaces, adventure to exalted murderers, romance to silly, mooning novels. Like the flower girl in Galsworthy's play, we have made a very considerable confusion of the life of joy and the joy of life. The first impulse is to abolish all lobster palaces, melodramas, yellow newspapers, and sentimentally erotic novels. Why not abolish all the devil's works? the reformer wonders. The answer is in history. It can't be done that way. It is impossible to abolish either with a law or an axe the desires of men. It is dangerous, explosively dangerous, to thwart them for any length of time. The Puritans tried to choke the craving for pleasure in early New England. They had no theaters, no dances, no festivals. They burned witches instead.

We rail a good deal against Tammany Hall. Reform

tickets make periodic sallies against it, crying economy, efficiency, and a business administration. And we all pretend to be enormously surprised when the "ignorant foreign vote" prefers a corrupt political ring to a party of well-dressed, grammatical, and high-minded gentlemen. Some of us are even rather downcast about democracy because the Bowery doesn't take to heart the admonitions of the Evening Post.

We forget completely the important wants supplied by Tammany Hall. We forget that this is a lonely country for an immigrant and that the Statue of Liberty doesn't shed her light with too much warmth. Possessing nothing but a statistical, inhuman conception of government, the average municipal reformer looks down contemptuously upon a man like Tim Sullivan with his clambakes and his dances; his warm and friendly saloons, his handshaking and funeral-going and baby-christening; his readiness to get coal for the family, and a job for the husband. But a Tim Sullivan is closer to the heart of statesmanship than five City Clubs full of people who want low taxes and orderly bookkeeping. He does things which have to be done. He humanizes a strange country; he is a friend at court; he represents the legitimate kindliness of government, standing between the poor and the impersonal, uninviting majesty of the law. Let no man wonder that Lorimer's people do not prefer an efficiency expert, that a Tim Sullivan has power, or that men are loyal to Hinky Dink. The cry raised against these men by the average reformer is a piece of cold, unreal, preposterous idealism compared to the solid warm facts of kindliness, clothes, food and fun.

The Taboo

You cannot beat the bosses with the reformer's taboo.
You will not get far on the Bowery with the cost unit system
and low taxes. And I don't blame the Bowery. You can beat
Tammany Hall permanently in one way—by making the
government of a city as human, as kindly, as jolly, as Tammany Hall. I am aware of the contract-grafts, the franchise—steals, the dirty streets, the bribing and the blackmail, the vice-and-crime partnerships, the Big Business
alliances of Tammany Hall. And yet it seems to me that
Tammany has a better perception of human need, and
comes nearer to being what a government should be, than
any scheme yet proposed by a group of "uptown good government" enthusiasts. Tammany is not a satanic instrument
of deception, cleverly devised to thwart "the will of the people." It is a crude and largely unconscious answer to certain
immediate needs, and without those needs its power would
crumble. That is why I ventured in the preceding chapter to
describe it as a natural sovereignty which had grown up
behind a mechanical form of government. It is a poor weed
compared to what government might be. But it is a real government that has power and serves a want, and not a frame
imposed upon men from on top.

The taboo—the merely negative law—is the emptiest of
all the impositions from on top. In its long record of failure,
in the comparative success of Tammany, those who are
aiming at social changes can see a profound lesson; the
impulses, cravings and wants of men must be employed.
You can employ them well or ill, but you must employ
them. A group of reformers lounging at a club cannot, dare
not, decide to close up another man's club because it is

[*51*]

called a saloon. Unless the reformer can invent something which substitutes attractive virtues for attractive vices, he will fail. He will fail because human nature abhors the vacuum created by the taboo.

An incident in the international peace propaganda illuminates this point. Not long ago a meeting in Carnegie Hall, New York, to forward peace among nations broke up in great disorder. Thousands of people who hate the waste and futility of war as much as any of the orators of that evening were filled with an unholy glee. They chuckled with delight at the idea of a riot in a peace meeting. Though it would have seemed perverse to the ordinary pacificist, this sentiment sprang from a respectable source. It had the same ground as the instinctive feeling of nine men in ten that Roosevelt has more right to talk about peace than William Howard Taft. James made it articulate in his essay on "The Moral Equivalent of War." James was a great advocate of peace, but he understood Theodore Roosevelt and he spoke for the military man when he wrote of war that: "Its 'horrors' are a cheap price to pay for rescue from the only alternative supposed, of a world of clerks and teachers, of co-education and zo-ophily, of 'consumers' leagues' and 'associated charities,' of industrialism unlimited, and feminism unabashed. No scorn, no hardness, no valor any more! Fie upon such a cattleyard of a planet!"

And he added: "So far as the central essence of this feeling goes, no healthy minded person, it seems to me, can help to some degree partaking of it. Militarism is the great preserver of our ideals of hardihood, and human life with no use for hardihood would be contemptible. Without risks or prizes for the darer, history would be insipid indeed; and there is a type of military character which everyone feels that the race should never cease to breed, for everyone is sensitive to its superiority."

So William James proposed not the abolition of war, but a moral equivalent for it. He dreamed of "a conscription of the whole youthful population to form for a certain number of years a part of the army enlisted against *Nature*. . . . The military ideals of hardihood and discipline would be wrought into the growing fibre of the people; no one would remain blind, as the luxurious classes now are blind, to man's relations to the globe he lives on, and to the permanently sour and hard foundations of his higher life." Now we are not concerned here over the question of this particular proposal. The telling point in my opinion is this: that when a wise man, a student of human nature, and a reformer met in the same person, the taboo was abandoned. James has given us a lasting phrase when he speaks of the "moral equivalent" of evil. We can use it, I believe, as a guide post to statesmanship. Rightly understood, the idea behind the words contains all that is valuable in conservatism, and, for the first time, gives a reputable meaning to that tortured epithet "constructive."

"The military feelings," says James, "are too deeply grounded to abdicate their place among our ideals until better substitutes are offered . . . such a conscription, with the state of public opinion that would have required it, and the many moral fruits it would bear, would preserve in the midst of a pacific civilization the manly virtues which the military party is so afraid of seeing disappear in peace. . . .

So far, war has been the only force that can discipline a whole community, and until an equivalent discipline is organized I believe that war must have its way. But I have no serious doubt that the ordinary prides and shames of social man, once developed to a certain intensity, are capable of organizing such a moral equivalent as I have sketched, or some other just as effective for preserving manliness of type. It is but a question of time, of skilful propagandism, and of opinion-making men seizing historic opportunities. The martial type of character can be bred without war."

To find for evil its moral equivalent is to be conservative about values and radical about forms, to turn to the establishment of positively good things instead of trying simply to check bad ones, to emphasize the additions to life, instead of the restrictions upon it, to substitute, if you like, the love of heaven for the fear of hell. Such a program means the dignified utilization of the whole nature of man. It will recognize as the first test of all political systems and moral codes whether or not they are "against human nature." It will insist that they be cut to fit the whole man, not merely a part of him. For there are utopian proposals made every day which cover about as much of a human being as a beautiful hat does.

Instead of tabooing our impulses, we must redirect them. Instead of trying to crush badness we must turn the power behind it to good account. The assumption is that every lust is capable of some civilized expression.

We say, in effect, that evil is a way by which desire expresses itself. The older moralists, the taboo philosophers believed that the desires themselves were inherently evil. To us they are the energies of the soul, neither good nor bad in themselves. Like dynamite, they are capable of all sorts of uses, and it is the business of civilization, through the family and the school, religion, art, science, and all institutions, to transmute these energies into fine values. Behind evil there is power, and it is folly,—wasting and disappointing folly,—to ignore this power because it has found an evil issue. All that is dynamic in human character is in these rooted lusts. The great error of the taboo has been just this: that it believed each desire had only one expression, that if that expression was evil the desire itself was evil. We know a little better to-day. We know that it is possible to harness desire to many interests, that evil is one form of a desire, and not the nature of it.

This supplies us with a standard for judging reforms, and so makes dear what "constructive" action really is. When it was discovered recently that the boys' gang was not an unmitigated nuisance to be chased by a policeman, but a force that could be made valuable to civilization through the Boy Scouts, a really constructive reform was given to the world. The effervescence of boys on the street, wasted and perverted through neglect or persecution, was drained and applied to fine uses. When Percy MacKaye pleads for pageants in which the people themselves participate, he offers an opportunity for expressing some of the lusts of the city in the form of an art. The Freudian school of psychologists calls this "sublimation." They have brought forward a wealth of material which gives us every reason to believe that the theory of "moral equivalents" is soundly based, that much the same energies produce crime and civilization, art, vice, insanity, love, lust, and religion. In each individual the original differences are small. Training and opportunity decide in the main how men's lust shall emerge. Left to themselves, or ignorantly tabooed, they break forth in some barbaric or morbid form. Only by supplying our passions with civilized interests can we escape their destructive force.

I have put it negatively, as a counsel of prudence. But he who has the courage of existence will put it triumphantly, crying "yea" as Nietzsche did, and recognizing that all the passions of men are the motive powers of a fine life.

For the roads that lead to heaven and hell are one until they part.

CHAPTER III

THE CHANGING FOCUS

THE taboo, however useless, is at least concrete. Although it achieves little besides mischief, it has all the appearance of practical action, and consequently enlists the enthusiasm of those people whom Wells describes as rushing about the country shouting: "For Gawd's sake let's *do* something *now*." There are weight and solidity in a policeman's club, while a "moral equivalent" happens to be pale like the stuff of which dreams are made. To the politician whose daily life consists in dodging the thousand and one conflicting prejudices of his constituents, in bickering with committees, intriguing and playing for the vote; to the business man harassed on four sides by the trust, the union, the law, and public opinion,—distrustful of any wide scheme because the stupidity of his shipping clerk is the most vivid item in his mind, all this discussion about politics and the inner life will sound like so much fine-spun nonsense.

I, for one, am not disposed to blame the politicians and the business men. They govern the nation, it is true, but they do it in a rather absentminded fashion. Those revolutionists who see the misery of the country as a deliberate and fiendish plot overestimate the bad will, the intelligence and the singleness of purpose in the ruling classes. Business and political leaders don't mean badly; the trouble with them is that most of the time they don't mean anything. They picture themselves as very "practical," which in practice amounts to saying that nothing makes them feel so spiritually homeless as the discussion of values and an invitation to examine first principles. Ideas, most of the time, cause them genuine distress, and are as disconcerting as an idle office boy, or a squeaky telephone.

I do not underestimate the troubles of the man of affairs. I have lived with politicians,—with socialist politicians whose good-will was abundant and intentions constructive. The petty vexations pile up into mountains; the distracting details scatter the attention and break up thinking, while the mere problem of exercising power crowds out speculation about what to do with it. Personal jealousies interrupt co-ordinated effort; committee sessions wear out nerves by their aimless drifting; constant speech-making turns a man back upon a convenient little store of platitudes—misunderstanding and distortion dry up the imagination, make thought timid and expression flat, the atmosphere of publicity requires a mask which soon becomes the reality. Politicians tend to live "in character," and many a public figure has come to imitate the journalism which describes him. You cannot blame politicians if their perceptions are few and their thinking crude.

Football strategy does not originate in a scrimmage: it is useless to expect solutions in a political campaign. Woodrow Wilson brought to public life an exceedingly flexible mind,—many of us when he first emerged rejoiced at the clean and athletic quality of his thinking. But even he under the stress of a campaign slackened into commonplace reiteration, accepting a futile and intellectually dishonest platform, closing his eyes to facts, misrepresenting his opponents, abandoning, in short, the very qualities which distinguished him. It is understandable. When a National Committee puts a megaphone to a man's mouth and tells him to yell, it is difficult for him to hear anything.

If a nation's destiny were really bound up with the politics reported in newspapers, the impasse would be discouraging. If the important sovereignty of a country were in what is called its parliamentary life, then the day of Plato's philosopher-kings would be far off indeed. Certainly nobody expects our politicians to become philosophers. When they do they hide the fact. And when philosophers try to be politicians they generally cease to be philosophers. But the truth is that we overestimate enormously the importance of nominations, campaigns, and office-holding. If we are discouraged it is because we tend to identify statecraft with that official government which is merely one of its instruments. Vastly overadvertised, we have mistaken an inflated fragment for the real political life of the country.

For if you think of men and their welfare, government appears at once as nothing but an agent among many others. The task of civilizing our impulses by creating fine opportunities for their expression cannot be accomplished through the City Hall alone. All the influences of social life are needed. The eggs do not lie in one basket. Thus the issues in the trade unions may be far more directly important to statecraft than the destiny of the Republican Party. The power that workingmen generate when they unite—the demands they will make and the tactics they will pursue—how they are educating themselves and the nation—these are genuine issues which bear upon the future. So with the policies of business men. Whether financiers are to be sullen and stupid like Archbold, defiant like Morgan, or well-intentioned like Perkins is a question that enters deeply into the industrial issues. The whole business problem takes on a new complexion if the representatives of capital are to be men with the temper of Louis Brandeis or William C. Redfield. For when business careers are made professional, new motives enter into the situation; it will make a world of difference if the leadership of industry is in the hands of men interested in production as a creative art instead of as a brute exploitation. The economic conflicts are at once raised to a plane of research, experiment and honest deliberation. For on the level of hate and mean—seeking no solution is possible. That subtle fact,—the change of business motives, the demonstration that industry can be conducted as medicine is,—may civilize the whole class conflict.

Obviously statecraft is concerned with such a change, extra-political though it is. And wherever the politician through his prestige or the government through its universities can stimulate a revolution in business motives, it should do so. That is genuinely constructive work, and will do more to a humane solution of the class struggle than all the jails and state constabularies that ever betrayed the barbarism of the Twentieth Century. It is no wonder that business is such a sordid affair. We have done our best to exclude from it every passionate interest that is capable of lighting up activity with eagerness and joy. "Unbusiness-like" we have called the devotion of craftsmen and scientists. We have actually pretended that the work of extracting a living from nature could be done most successfully by shortsighted money-makers encouraged by their money-spending wives. We are learning better to-day. We are beginning to know that this nation for all its boasts has not touched the real possibilities of business success, that nature and good luck have done most of our work, that our achievements come in spite of our ignorance. And so no man can gauge the civilizing possibilities of a new set of motives in business. That it will add to the dignity and value of millions of careers is only one of its blessings. Given a nation of men trained to think scientifically about their work and feel about it as craftsmen, and you have a people released from a stupid fixation upon the silly little ideals of accumulating dollars and filling their neighbor's eye. We preach against commercialism but without great result. And the reason for our failure is: that we merely say "you ought not" instead of offering a new interest. Instead of telling business men not to be greedy, we should tell them to be industrial statesmen, applied scientists, and members of a craft. Politics can aid that revolution in a hundred ways: by advocating it, by furnishing schools that teach, laboratories that demonstrate, by putting business on the same plane of interest as the Health Service.

The indictment against politics to-day is not its corruption, but its lack of insight. I believe it is a fact which experience will sustain that men steal because they haven't anything better to do. You don't have to preach honesty to men with a creative purpose. Let a human being throw the energies of his soul into the making of something, and the instinct of workmanship will take care of his honesty. The writers who have nothing to say are the ones that you can buy: the others have too high a price. A genuine craftsman will not adulterate his product: the reason isn't because duty says he shouldn't, but because passion says he couldn't. I suggested in an earlier chapter that the issue of honesty and dishonesty was a futile one, and I placed faith in the creative men. They hate shams and the watering of goods on a more trustworthy basis than the mere routine moralist. To them dishonesty is a contradiction of their own lusts, and they ask no credit, need none, for being true. Creation is an emotional ascent, which makes the standard vices trivial, and turns all that is valuable in virtue to the service of desire.

When politics revolves mechanically it ceases to use the real energies of a nation. Government is then at once irrelevant and mischievous—a mere obstructive nuisance. Not long ago a prominent senator remarked that he didn't know much about the country, because he had spent the last few months in Washington. It was a profound utterance as anyone can testify who reads, let us say, the Congressional Record. For that document, though replete with language, is singularly unacquainted with the forces that agitate the nation. Politics, as the contributors to the Congressional Record seem to understand it, is a very limited selection of well-worn debates on a few arbitrarily chosen "problems." Those questions have developed a technique and an interest in them for their own sake. They are handled with a dull solemnity quite out of proportion to their real interest.

Labor receives only a perfunctory and largely disingenuous attention; even commerce is handled in a way that expresses neither its direction nor its public use. Congress has been ready enough to grant favors to corporations, but where in its wrangling from the Sherman Act to the Commerce Court has it shown any sympathetic understanding of the constructive purposes in the trust movement? It has either presented the business man with money or harassed him with bungling enthusiasm in the pretended interests of the consumer. The one thing Congress has not done is to use the talents of business men for the nation's advantage.

If "politics" has been indifferent to forces like the union and the trust, it is no exaggeration to say that it has displayed a modest ignorance of women's problems, of educational conflicts and racial aspirations; of the control of newspapers and magazines, the book publishing world, socialist conventions and unofficial political groups like the single-taxers.

Such genuine powers do not absorb our political interest because we are fooled by the regalia of office. But statesmanship, if it is to be relevant, would obtain a new perspective on these dynamic currents, would find out the wants they express and the energies they contain, would shape and direct and guide them. For unions and trusts, sects, clubs and voluntary associations stand for actual needs. The size of their following, the intensity of their demands are a fair index of what the statesman must think about. No lawyer created a trust though he drew up its charter; no logician made the labor movement or the feminist agitation. If you ask what for political purposes a nation is, a practical answer would be: it is its "movements." They are the social *life*. So far as the future is man-made it is made of them. They show their real vitality by a relentless growth in spite of all the little fences and obstacles that foolish politicians devise.

There is, of course, much that is dead within the movements. Each one carries along a quantity of inert and outworn ideas,—not infrequently there is an internally contradictory current. Thus the very workingmen who agitate for a better diffusion of wealth display a marked hostility to improvements in the production of it. The feminists too have their atavisms: not a few who object to the patriarchal family seem inclined to cure it by going back still more—to the matriarchal. Constructive business has no end of reactionary moments—the most striking, perhaps, is when it buys up patents in order to suppress them. Yet these inversions, though discouraging, are not essential in the life of movements. They need to be expurgated by an unceasing criticism; yet in bulk the forces I have mentioned, and many others less important, carry with them the creative powers of our times.

It is not surprising that so many political inventions have been made within these movements, fostered by them, and brought to a general public notice through their efforts. When some constructive proposal is being agitated before a legislative committee, it is customary to unite the "movements" in support of it. Trade unions and women's clubs have joined hands in many an agitation. There are proposals to-day, like the minimum wage, which seem sure of support from consumers' leagues, women's federations, trade unions and those far-sighted business men who may be called "State Socialists."

In fact, unless a political invention is woven into a social movement it has no importance. Only when that is done is it imbued with life. But how among countless suggestions is a "cause" to know the difference between a true invention and a pipe-dream? There is, of course, no infallible touchstone by which we can tell offhand. No one need hope for an easy certainty either here or anywhere else in human affairs. No one is absolved from experiment and constant revision. Yet there are some hypotheses that prima facie deserve more attention than others.

Those are the suggestions which come out of a recognized human need. If a man proposed that the judges of the Supreme Court be reduced from nine to seven because the number seven has mystical power, we could ignore him. But if he suggested that the number be reduced because seven men can deliberate more effectively than nine he ought to be given a hearing. Or let us suppose that the argument is about granting votes to women. The suffragist who bases a claim on the so-called "logic of democracy" is making the poorest possible showing for a good cause. I have heard people maintain that: "it makes no difference whether women want the ballot, or are fit for it, or can do any good with it,—this country is a democracy. Democracy means government by the votes of the people. Women are people. Therefore women should vote." That in a very simple form is the mechanical conception of government. For notice how it ignores human wants and human powers—how it subordinates people to a rigid formula. I use this crude example because it shows that even the most genuine and deeply grounded demands are as yet unable to free themselves entirely from a superficial manner of thinking. We are only partially emancipated from the mechanical and merely logical tradition of the Eighteenth Century. No end of illustrations could be adduced. In the Socialist party it has been the custom to denounce the "short ballot." Why? Because it reduces the number of elective offices. This is regarded as undemocratic for the reason that democracy has come to mean a series of elections. According to a logic, the more elections the more democratic. But experience has shown that a seven-foot ballot with a regiment of names is so bewildering that a real choice is impossible. So it is proposed to cut down the number of elective offices, focus the attention on a few alternatives, and turn voting into a fairly intelligent performance. Here is an attempt to fit political devices to the actual powers of the voter. The old, crude form of ballot forgot that finite beings had to operate it. But the "democrats" adhere to the multitude of choices because "logic" requires them to.

This incident of the "short ballot" illustrates the cleavage between invention and routine. The socialists oppose it not because their intentions are bad but because on this issue their thinking is mechanical. Instead of applying the test of human need, they apply a verbal and logical consistency. The "short ballot" in itself is a slight affair, but the insight behind it seems to me capable of revolutionary development. It is one symptom of the effort to found institutions on human nature. There are many others.

We might point to the first experiments aimed at remedying the helter-skelter of careers by vocational guidance. Carried through successfully, this invention of Prof. Parsons' is one whose significance in happiness can hardly be exaggerated. When you think of the misfits among your acquaintances—the lawyers who should be mechanics, the doctors who should be business men, the teachers who should have been clerks, and the executives who should be doing research in a laboratory—when you think of the talent that would be released by proper use, the imagination takes wing at the possibilities. What could we not make of the world if we employed its genius!

Whoever is working to express special energies is part of a constructive revolution. Whoever is removing the stunting environments of our occupations is doing the fundamentals of reform. The studies of Miss Goldmark of industrial fatigue, recuperative power and maximum productivity are contributions toward that distant and desirable period when labor shall be a free and joyous activity. Every suggestion which turns work from a drudgery to a craft is worth our deepest interest. For until then the labor problem will never be solved. The socialist demand for a better distribution of wealth is of great consequence, but without a change in the very nature of labor society will not have achieved the happiness it expects. That is why imaginative socialists have shown so great an interest in "syndicalism." There at least in some of its forms, we can catch sight of a desire to make all labor a self-governing craft.

The handling of crime has been touched by the modern impetus. The ancient, abstract and wholesale "justice" is breaking up into detailed and carefully adapted treatment of individual offenders. What this means for the child has become common knowledge in late years. Criminology (to use an awkward word) is finding a human center. So is education. Everyone knows how child study is revolutionizing the school room and the curriculum. Why, it seems that Mme. Montessori has had the audacity to sacrifice the sacred bench to the interests of the pupil! The traditional school seems to be vanishing—that place in which an ill-assorted band of youngsters was for a certain number of hours each day placed in the vicinity of a text-book and a maiden lady.

I mention these experiments at random. It is not the specific reforms that I wish to emphasize but the great possibilities they foreshadow. Whether or not we adopt certain special bills, high tariff or low tariff, one banking system or another, this trust control or that, is a slight gain compared to a change of attitude toward all political problems. The reformer bound up in his special propaganda will, of course, object that "to get something done is worth more than any amount of talk about new ways of looking at political problems." What matters the method, he will cry, provided the reform be good? Well, the method matters more than any particular reform. A man who couldn't think straight might get the right answer to one problem, but how much faith would you have in his capacity to solve the next one? If you wanted to educate a child, would you teach him to read one play of Shakespeare, or would you teach him to *read*? If the world were going to remain frigidly set after next year, we might well thank our stars if we blundered into a few decent solutions right away. But as there is no prospect of a time when our life will be immutably fixed, as we shall, therefore, have to go on inventing, it is fair to say that what the world is aching for is not a special reform embodied in a particular statute, but a way of going at all problems. The lasting value of Darwin, for example, is not in any concrete conclusion he reached. His importance to the world lies in the new twist he gave to science. He lent it fruitful direction, a different impetus, and the results are beyond his imagining.

In that spiritual autobiography of a searching mind, "The New Machiavelli," Wells describes his progress from a reformer of concrete abuses to a revolutionist in method. "You see," he says, "I began in my teens by wanting to plan and build cities and harbors for mankind; I ended in the middle thirties by desiring only to serve and increase a general process of thought, a process fearless, critical, real-spirited, that would in its own time give cities, harbors, air, happiness, everything at a scale and quality and in a light altogether beyond the match-striking imaginations of a contemporary mind. . . ."

This same veering of interest may be seen in the career of another Englishman. I refer to Mr. Graham Wallas. Back in the '80's he was working with the Webbs, Bernard Shaw, Sidney Olivier, Annie Besant and others in socialist propaganda. Readers of the Fabian Essays know Mr. Wallas and appreciate the work of his group. Perhaps more than anyone else, the Fabians are responsible for turning English socialist thought from the verbalism of the Marxian disciples to the actualities of English political life. Their appetite for the concrete was enormous; their knowledge of facts overpowering, as the tomes produced by Mr. and Mrs. Webb can testify. The socialism of the Fabians soon became a definite legislative program which the various political parties were to be bulldozed, cajoled and tricked into enacting. It was effective work, and few can question the value of it. Yet many admirers have been left with a sense of inadequacy.

Unlike the orthodox socialists, the Fabians took an active part in immediate politics. "We permeated the party organizations," writes Shaw, "and pulled all the wires we could lay our hands on with our utmost adroitness and energy. . . . The generalship of this movement was undertaken chiefly by Sidney Webb, who played such bewildering conjuring tricks with the Liberal thimbles and the Fabian peas that to this day both the Liberals and the sectarian Socialists stand aghast at him." Few Americans know how great has been this influence on English political history for the last twenty years. The well-known Minority Report of the Poor Law Commission bears the Webb signature most conspicuously. Fabianism began to achieve a reputation for getting things done—for taking part in "practical affairs." Bernard Shaw has found time to do no end of campaigning and even the parochial politics of a vestryman has not seemed too insignificant for his Fabian enthusiasm. Graham Wallas was a candidate in five municipal elections, and has held an important office as member of the London County Council.

But the original Fabian enthusiasm has slackened. One might ascribe it to a growing sense that concrete programs by themselves will not insure any profound regeneration of society. H. G. Wells has been savage and often unfair about the Fabian Society, but in "The New Machiavelli" he touched, I believe, the real disillusionment. Remington's history is in a way symbolic. Here was a successful political reformer, coming more and more to a disturbing recognition of his helplessness, perceiving the aimlessness and the unreality of political life, and announcing his contempt for the "crudification" of all issues. What Remington missed was what so many reformers are beginning to miss—an underlying philosophical habit.

Mr. Wallas seems to have had much the same experience. In the midst of a bustle of activity, politics appeared to have no center to which its thinking and doing could be referred. The truth was driven home upon him that political science is a science of human relationship with the human beings left out. So he writes that "the thinkers of the past, from Plato to Bentham and Mill, had each his own view of human nature, and they made these views the basis of their speculations on government." But to-day "nearly all students of politics analyze institutions and avoid the analysis of man." Whoever has read the typical book on politics by a professor or a reformer will agree, I think, when he adds: "One feels that many of the more systematic books on politics by American University professors are useless, just because the writers dealt with abstract men, formed on assumptions of which they were unaware and which they have never tested either by experience or by study."

An extreme example could be made of Nicholas Murray Butler, President of Columbia University. In the space of six months he wrote an impassioned defense of "constitutional government," beginning with the question, "Why is it that in the United States the words politics and politician have associations that are chiefly of evil omen," and then, to make irony complete, proceeded at the New York State Republican Convention to do the jobbery of Boss Barnes. What is there left but to gasp and wonder whether the words of the intellect have anything to do with the facts of life? What insight into reality can a man possess who is capable of discussing politics and ignoring politicians? What kind of naïveté was it that led this educator into asking such a question?

President Butler is, I grant, a caricature of the typical professor. Yet what shall we say of the annual harvest of treatises on "labor problems" which make no analysis of the mental condition of laboring men; of the treatises on marriage and prostitution which gloss over the sexual life of the individual? "In the other sciences which deal with human affairs," writes Mr. Wallas, referring to pedagogy and criminology, "this division between the study of the thing done and the study of the being who does it is not found."

I have in my hands a text-book of six hundred pages which is used in the largest universities as a groundwork of political economy. This remarkable sentence strikes the eye: "The motives to business activity are too familiar to require analysis." But some sense that perhaps the "economic man" is not a self-evident creature seems to have touched our author. So we are treated to these sapient remarks: "To avoid this criticism we will begin with a characterization of the typical business man to be found to-day in the United States and other countries in the same stage of industrial development. *He has four traits which show themselves more or less clearly in all of his acts.*" They are first "self-interest," but "this does not mean that he is steeped in selfishness . . ."; secondly, "the larger self," the family, union, club, and "in times of emergency his country"; thirdly, "love of independence," for "his ambition is to stand on his own feet"; fourthly, "business ethics" which "are not usually as high as the standards professed in churches, but they are much higher than current criticisms of business would lead one to think." Three-quarters of a page is sufficient for this penetrating analysis of motive and is followed by the remark that "these four characteristics of the ecocomic man are readily explained by reference to the evolutionary process which has brought industrial society to its present stage of development."

If those were the generalizations of a tired business man after a heavy dinner and a big cigar, they would still seem rather muddled and useless. But as the basis of an economic treatise in which "laws" are announced, "principles" laid down, reforms criticized as "impracticable," all for the benefit of thousands of college students, it is hardly possible to exaggerate the folly of such an exhibition. I have taken a book written by one eminent professor and evidently approved by others, for they use it as a text-book. It is no queer freak. I myself was supposed to read that book pretty nearly every week for a year. With hundreds of others I was supposed to found my economic understanding upon it. We were actually punished for not reading that book. It was given to us as wisdom, as modern political economy.

But what goes by the name to-day is a potpourri in which one can distinguish descriptions of legal forms, charters and institutions; comparative studies of governmental and social machinery; the history of institutions, a few "principles" like the law of rent, some moral admonitions, a good deal of class feeling, not a little timidity—but almost no attempt to cut beneath these manifestations of social life to the creative impulses which produce them. The Economic Man—that lazy abstraction—is still paraded in the lecture room; the study of human nature has not advanced beyond the gossip of old wives.

Graham Wallas touched the cause of the trouble when he pointed out that political science to-day discusses institutions and ignores the nature of the men who make and live under them. I have heard professors reply that it wasn't their business to discuss human nature but to record and interpret economic and political facts. Yet if you probe those "interpretations" there is no escaping the conclusion that they rest upon some notion of what man is like. "The student of politics," writes Mr. Wallas, "must, consciously or unconsciously, form a conception of human nature, and the less conscious he is of his conception the more likely he is to be dominated by it." For politics is an interest of men—a tool which they fabricate and use—and no comment has much value if it tries to get along without mankind. You might as well try to describe food by ignoring the digestion.

Mr. Wallas has called a halt. I think we may say that his is the distinction of having turned the study of politics back to the humane tradition of Plato and Machiavelli—of having made man the center of political investigation. The very title of his book—"Human Nature in Politics"—is significant. Now in making that statement, I am aware that it is a sweeping one, and I do not mean to imply that Mr. Wallas is the only modern man who has tried to think about politics psychologically. Here in America alone we have two splendid critics, a man and a woman, whose thought flows from an interpretation of human character. Thorstein Veblen's brilliant descriptions penetrate deeply into our mental life, and Jane Addams has given new hope to many of us by her capacity for making ideals the goal of natural desire.

Nor is it just to pass by such a suggestive thinker as Gabriel Tarde, even though we may feel that his psychology is too simple and his conclusions somewhat overdriven by a favorite theory. The work of Gustav Le Bon on "crowds" has, of course, passed into current thought, but I doubt whether anyone could say that he had even prepared a basis for a new political psychology. His own aversion to reform, his fondness for vast epochs and his contempt for current effort have left most of his "psychological laws" in the region of interesting literary comment. There are, too, any number of "social psychologies," such as those of Ross and McDougall. But the trouble with them is that the "psychology" is weak and uninformed, distorted by moral enthusiasms, and put out without any particular reference to the task of statesmanship. When you come to special problems, the literature of the subject picks up. Crime is receiving valuable attention, education is profoundly affected, alcoholism and sex have been handled for a good while on a psychological basis.

But it remained for Mr. Wallas to state the philosophy of the matter—to say why the study of human nature must serve politics, and to point out how. He has not produced a political psychology, but he has written the manifesto for it. As a result, fragmentary investigations can be brought together and applied to the work of statecraft. Merely by making these researches self-conscious, he has made clearer their goal, given them direction, and kindled them to practical action. How necessary this work is can be seen in the writing of Miss Addams. Owing to keen insight and fine sympathy her thinking has generally been on a human basis. Yet Miss Addams is a reformer, and sympathy without an explicit philosophy may lead to a distorted enthusiasm. Her book on prostitution seems rather the product of her moral fervor than her human insight. Compare it with "The Spirit of Youth" or "Newer Ideals of Peace" or "Democracy and Social Ethics" and I think you will notice a very considerable willingness to gloss over human need in the interests of an unanalyzed reform. To put it bluntly, Miss Addams let her impatience get the better of her wisdom. She had written brilliantly about sex and its "sublimation," she had suggested notable "moral equivalents" for vice, but when she touched the white slave traffic its horrors were so great that she also put her faith in the policeman and the district attorney. "A New Conscience and an Ancient Evil" is an hysterical book, just because the real philosophical basis of Miss Addams' thinking was not delibcrate enough to withstand the shock of a poignant horror.

It is this weakness that Mr. Wallas comes to remedy. He has described what political science must be like, and anyone who has absorbed his insight has an intellectual groundwork for political observation. No one, least of all Mr. Wallas, would claim anything like finality for the essay. These labors are not done in a day. But he has deliberately brought the study of politics to the only focus which has any rational interest for mankind. He has made a plea, and sketched a plan which hundreds of investigators the world over must help to realize. If political science could travel in the direction suggested, its criticism would be relevant, its proposals practical. There would, for the first time, be a concerted effort to build a civilization around mankind, to use its talent and to satisfy its needs. There would be no more empty taboos, no erecting of institutions upon abstract and mechanical analogies. Politics would be like education—an effort to develop, train and nurture men's impulses. As Montessori is building the school around the child, so politics would build all of social life around the human being.

That practical issues hang upon these investigations can be shown by an example from Mr. Wallas's book. Take the quarrel over socialism. You hear it said that without the private ownership of capital people will lose ambition and sink into sloth. Many men, just as well aware of present-day evils as the socialists, are unwilling to accept the collectivist remedy. G. K. Chesterton and Hilaire Belloc speak of the "magic of property" as the real obstacle to socialism. Now obviously this is a question of first-rate importance. If socialism will destroy initiative then only a doctrinaire would desire it. But how is the question to be solved? You cannot reason it out. Economics, as we know it to-day, is quite incapable of answering such a problem, for it is a matter that depends upon psychological investigation. When a professor says that socialism is impracticable he begs the question, for that amounts to assuming that the point at issue is already settled. If he tells you that socialism is against human nature, we have a perfect right to ask where he proved the possibilities of human nature.

But note how Mr. Wallas approaches the debate: "Children quarrel at furiously at a very early age over apparently worthless things, and collect and hide them long before they can have any clear notion of the advantages to be derived from individual possession. Those children who in certain charity schools are brought up entirely without personal property, even in their clothes or pocket handkerchiefs, show every sign of the bad effect on health and character which results from complete inability to satisfy a strong inherited instinct. . . . Some economist ought therefore to give us a treatise in which this property instinct is carefully and quantitatively examined. . . . How far can it be eliminated or modified by education? Is it satisfied by a leasehold or a life-interest, or by such an arrangement of corporate property as is offered by a collegiate foundation, or by the provision of a public park? Does it require for its satisfaction material and visible things such as land or houses, or is the holding, say, of colonial railway shares sufficient? Is the absence of unlimited proprietary rights felt more strongly in the case of personal chattels (such as furniture and ornaments) than in the case of land or machinery? Does the degree and direction of the instinct markedly differ among different individuals or races, or between the two sexes?"

This puts the argument upon a plane where discussion is relevant. This is no trumped-up issue: it is asked by a politician and a socialist seeking for a real solution. We need to know whether the "magic of property" extends from a man's garden to Standard Oil stocks as anti-socialists say, and, conversely, we need to know what is happening to that mass of proletarians who own no property and cannot satisfy their instincts even with personal chattels.

For if ownership is a human need, we certainly cannot taboo it as the extreme communists so dogmatically urge. "Pending . . . an inquiry," writes Mr. Wallas, "my own provisional opinion is that, like a good many instincts of very early evolutionary origin, it can be satisfied by an avowed pretense; just as a kitten which is fed regularly on milk can be kept in good health if it is allowed to indulge its hunting instinct by playing with a bobbin, and a peaceful civil servant satisfies his instinct of combat and adventure at golf."

Mr. Wallas takes exactly the same position as William James did when he planned a "moral equivalent" for war. Both men illustrate the changing focus of political thought. Both try to found statesmanship on human need. Both see that there are good and bad satisfactions of the same impulse. The routineer with his taboo does not see this, so he attempts the impossible task of obliterating the impulse. He differs fundamentally from the creative politician who devotes himself to inventing fine expressions for human needs, who recognizes that the work of statesmanship is in large measure the finding of good substitutes for the bad things we want.

This is the heart of a political revolution. When we recognize that the focus of politics is shifting from a mechanical to a human center we shall have reached what is, I believe, the most essential idea in modern politics. More than any other generalization it illuminates the currents of our national life and explains the altering tasks of statesmanship.

The old effort was to harness mankind to abstract principles—liberty, justice or equality—and to deduce institutions from these high-sounding words. It did not succeed because human nature was contrary and restive. The new effort proposes to fit creeds and institutions to the wants of men, to satisfy their impulses as fully and beneficially as possible.

And yet we do not begin to know our desires or the art of their satisfaction. Mr. Wallas's book and the special literature of the subject leave no doubt that a precise political psychology is far off indeed. The human nature we must put at the center of our statesmanship is only partially understood. True, Mr. Wallas works with a psychology that is fairly well superseded. But not even the advance-guard to-day, what we may call the Freudian school, would claim that it had brought knowledge to a point where politics could use it in any very deep or comprehensive way. The subject is crude and fragmentary, though we are entitled to call it promising.

Yet the fact had better be faced: psychology has not gone far enough, its results are still too vague for our purposes. We know very little, and what we know has hardly been applied to political problems. That the last few years have witnessed a revolution in the study of mental life is plain: the effects are felt not only in psychotherapy, but in education, morals, religion, and no end of cultural interests. The impetus of Freud is perhaps the greatest advance ever made towards the understanding and control of human character. But for the complexities of politics it is not yet ready. It will take time and endless labor for a detailed study of social problems in the light of this growing knowledge.

What then shall we do now? Must we continue to muddle along in the old ruts, gazing rapturously at an impotent ideal, until the works of the scientists are matured?

CHAPTER IV

THE GOLDEN RULE
AND AFTER

I T would indeed be an intolerably pedantic performance for a nation to sit still and wait for its scientists to report on their labors. The notion is typical of the pitfalls in the path of any theorist who does not correct his logic by a constant reference to the movement of life. It is true that statecraft must make human nature its basis. It is true that its chief task is the invention of forms and institutions which satisfy the inner needs of mankind. And it is true that our knowledge of those needs and the technique of their satisfaction is hazy, unorganized and blundering.

But to suppose that the remedy lies in waiting for monographs from the research of the laboratory is to have lost a sense of the rhythm of actual affairs. That is not the way things come about: we grow into a new point of view: only afterwards, in looking back, do we see the landmarks of our progress. Thus it is customary to say that Adam Smith dates the change from the old mercantilist economy to the capitalistic economics of the nineteenth century. But that is a manner of speech. The old mercantilist policy was giving way to early industrialism: a thousand unconscious economic and social forces were compelling the change. Adam Smith expressed the process, named it, idealized it and made it self-conscious. Then because men were clearer about what they were doing, they could in a measure direct their destiny.

That is but another way of saying that great revolutionary changes do not spring full-armed from anybody's brow. A genius usually becomes the luminous center of a nation's crisis,—men see better by the light of him. His bias deflects their actions. Unquestionably the doctrine-driven men who made the economics of the last century had much to do with the halo which encircled the smutted head of industrialism. They put the stamp of their genius on certain inhuman practices, and of course it has been the part of the academic mind to imitate them ever since. The orthodox economists are in the unenviable position of having taken their morals from the exploiter and of having translated them into the grandiloquent language of high public policy. They gave capitalism the sanction of the intellect. When later, Carlyle and Ruskin battered the economists into silence with invective and irony they were voicing the dumb protest of the humane people of England. They helped to organize a formless resentment by endowing it with intelligence and will.

So it is to-day. If this nation did not show an unmistakable tendency to put men at the center of politics instead of machinery and things; if there were not evidence to prove that we are turning from the sterile taboo to the creation of finer environments; if the impetus for shaping our destiny were not present in our politics and our life, then essays like these would be so much baying at the moon, fantastic and unworthy pleas for some irrelevant paradise. But the gropings are there,—vastly confused in the tangled strains of the nation's interests. Clogged by the confusion, half-choked by stupid blockades, largely unaware of their own purposes, it is for criticism, organized research, and artistic expression to free and to use these creative energies. They are to be found in the aspirations of labor, among the awakened women, in the development of business, the diffusion of art and science, in the racial mixtures, and many lesser interests which cluster about these greater movements.

The desire for a human politics is all about us. It rises to the surface in slogans like "human rights above property rights," "the man above the dollar." Some measure of its strength is given by the widespread imitation these expressions have compelled: politicians who haven't the slightest intention of putting men above the dollar, who if they had wouldn't know how, take off their hats to the sentiment because it seems a key to popular enthusiasm. It must be bewildering to men brought up, let us say, in the Hanna school of politics. For here is this nation which sixteen years ago vibrated ecstatically to that magic word "Prosperity"; to-day statistical rhetoric about size induces little but excessive boredom. If you wish to drive an audience out of the hall tell it how rich America is; if you wish to stamp yourself an echo of the past talk to us young men about the Republican Party's understanding with God in respect to bumper crops. But talk to us about "human rights," and though you talk rubbish, we'll listen. For our desire is bent that way, and anything which has the flavor of this new interest will rivet our attention. We are still uncritical. It is only a few years since we began to center our politics upon human beings. We have no training in that kind of thought. Our schools and colleges have helped us hardly at all. We still talk about "humanity" as if it were some strange and mystical creature which could not possibly be composed of the grocer, the street-car conductor and our aunts.

That the opinion-making people of America are more interested in human welfare than in empire or abstract prosperity is an item that no statesman can disregard in his thinking. To-day it is no longer necessary to run against the grain of the deepest movements of our time. There is an ascendant feeling among the people that all achievement should be measured in human happiness. This feeling has not always existed. Historians tell us that the very idea of progress in well-being is not much older than, say, Shakespeare's plays. As a general belief it is still more recent. The nineteenth century may perhaps be said to mark its popularization. But as a fact of immediate politics, as a touchstone applied quickly to all the acts of statecraft in America it belongs to the Twentieth Century. There were any number of people who long before 1900 saw that dollars and men could dash. But their insight had not won any general acceptance. It is only within the last few years that the human test has ceased to be the property of a small group and become the convention of a large majority. A study of magazines and newspapers would confirm this rather broad generalization. It would show, I believe, how the whole quality of our most impromptu thinking is being influenced by human values.

The Golden Rule and After

The statesman must look to this largely unorganized drift of desire. He will find it clustering about certain big revolts—the unrest of women, for example, or the increasing demands of industrial workers. Rightly understood, these social currents would, I believe, lead to the central issues of life, the vital points upon which happiness depends. They come out of necessities. They express desire. They are power.

Thus feminism, arising out of a crisis in sexual conditions, has liberated energies that are themselves the motors of any reform. In England and America voting has become the symbol of an aspiration as yet half-conscious and undefined. What women want is surely something a great deal deeper than the privilege of taking part in elections. They are looking for a readjustment of their relations to the home, to work, to children, to men, to the interests of civilized life. The vote has become a convenient peg upon which to hang aspirations that are not at all sure of their own meaning. In no insignificant number of cases the vote is a cover by which revolutionary demands can be given a conventional front. The ballot is at the utmost a beginning, as farsighted conservatives have guessed. Certainly the elimination of "male" from the suffrage qualifications will not end the feminist agitation. From the angle of statecraft the future of the movement may be said to depend upon the wise use of this raw and scattered power. I do not pretend to know in detail how this can be done. But I am certain that the task of leadership is to organize aspiration in the service of the real interests of life. To-day women want—what? They are ready to want something: that describes fairly the condition of most suffragettes. Those who like Ellen Key and Olive Shreiner and Mrs. Gilman give them real problems to think about are drafting that energy into use. By real problems I mean problems of love, work, home, children. They are the real interests of feminism because they have produced it.

The yearnings of to-day are the symptoms of needs, they point the course of invention, they are the energies which animate a social program. The most ideally conceived plan of the human mind has only a slight interest if it does not harness these instinctive forces. That is the great lesson which the utopias teach by their failure—that schemes, however nicely arranged, cannot be imposed upon human beings who are interested in other things. What ailed Don Quixote was that he and his contemporaries wanted different things; the only ideals that count are those which express the possible development of an existing force. Reformers must never forget that three legs are a Quixotic ideal; two good legs a genuine one.

In actual life, yes, in the moil and toil of propaganda, "movements," "causes" and agitations the statesman-inventor and the political psychologist find the raw material for their work. It is not the business of the politician to preserve an Olympian indifference to what stupid people call "popular whim." Being lofty about the "passing fad" and the ephemeral outcry is all very well in the biographies of dead men, but rank nonsense in the rulers of real ones. Oscar Wilde once remarked that only superficial people disliked the superficial. Nothing, for example, could on the surface be more trivial than an interest in baseball scores. Yet during the campaign of 1912 the excitement was so great that Woodrow Wilson said on the stump he felt like apologizing to the American people for daring to be a presidential candidate while the Giants and the Red Sox were playing for the championship. Baseball (not so much for those who play it), is a colossal phenomenon in American life. Watch the crowds in front of a bulletin board, finding a vicarious excitement and an abstract relief from the monotony of their own lives. What a second-hand civilization it is that grows passionate over a scoreboard with little electric lights! What a civilization it is that has learned to enjoy its sport without even seeing it! If ever there was a symptom that this nation needed leisure and direct participation in games, it is that poor scrawny substitute for joy—the baseball extra.

It is as symptomatic as the labor union. It expresses need. And statesmanship would find an answer. It would not let that passion and loyalty be frittered away to drift like scum through the nation. It would see in it the opportunity of art, play, and religion. So with what looks very different—the "syndicalist movement." Perhaps it seems preposterous to discuss baseball and syndicalism in the same paragraph. But that is only because we have not accustomed ourselves to thinking of social events as answers to human needs. The statesman would ask, Why are there syndicalists? What are they driving at? What gift to civilization is in the impetus behind them? They are human beings, and they want human things. There is no reason to become terror-stricken about them. They seem to want things badly. Then ostriches disguised as judges cannot deal with them. Anarchism—men die for that, they undergo intolerable insults. They are tarred and feathered and spat upon. Is it possible that Republicans, Democrats and Socialists clip the wings more than free spirits can allow? Is civilization perhaps too tightly organized? Have the irreconcilables a soul audacious and less blunted than our domesticated ones? To put it mildly, is it ever safe to ignore them entirely in our thinking?

We shall come, I think, to a different appraisal of agitations. Our present method is to discuss whether the proposals are right and feasible. We do this hastily and with prejudice. Generally we decide that any agitation foreign to our settled habits is wrong. And we bolster up our satisfaction by pointing to some mistake of logic or some puerility of statement. That done, we feel the agitation is deplorable and can be ignored unless it becomes so obstreperous that we have to put it in jail. But a genuine statecraft would go deeper. It would know that even God has been defended with nonsense. So it could be sympathetic to agitations. I use the word sympathetic literally. For it would try to understand the inner feeling which had generated what looks like a silly demand. To-day it is as if a hungry man asked for an indigestible food, and we let him go hungry because he was unwise. He isn't any the less hungry because he asks for the wrong food. So with agitations. Their specific plans may be silly, but their demands are real. The hungers and lusts of mankind have produced some stupendous follies, but the desires themselves are no less real and insistent.

The important thing about a social movement is not its stated platform but the source from which it flows. The task of politics is to understand those deeper demands and to find civilized satisfactions for them. The meaning of this is that the statesman must be more than the leader of a party. Thus the socialist statesman is not complete if he is a good socialist. Only the delusion that his truth is the whole truth, his party the human race, and his program a panacea, will produce that singleness of vision.

The moment a man takes office he has no right to be the representative of one group alone. He has assumed the burden of harmonizing particular agitations with the general welfare. That is why great agitators should not accept office. Men like Debs understand that. Their business is to make social demands so concrete and pressing that statesmen are forced to deal with them. Agitators who accept government positions are a disappointment to their followers. They can no longer be severely partisan. They have to look at affairs nationally. Now the agitator and the statesman are both needed. But they have different functions, and it is unjust to damn one because he hasn't the virtues of the other.

The statesman to-day needs a large equipment. The man who comes forward to shape a country's policy has truly no end of things to consider. He must be aware of the condition of the people: no statesman must fall into the sincere but thoroughly upper class blunder that President Taft committed when he advised a three months' vacation. Realizing how men and women feel at all levels and at different places, he must speak their discontent and project their hopes. Through this he will get power. Standing upon the prestige which that gives he must guide and purify the social demands he finds at work. He is the translator of agitations. For this task he must be keenly sensitive to public opinion and capable of understanding the dynamics of it. Then, in order to fuse it into a civilized achievement, he will require much expert knowledge. Yet he need not be a specialist himself, if only he is expert in choosing experts. It is better indeed that the statesman should have a lay, and not a professional view. For the bogs of technical stupidity and empty formalism are always near and always dangerous. The real political genius stands between the actual life of men, their wishes and their needs, and all the windings of official caste and professional snobbery. It is his supreme business to see that the servants of life stay in their place— that government, industry, "causes," science, all the creatures of man do not succeed in their perpetual effort to become the masters.

I have Roosevelt in mind. He haunts political thinking. And indeed, why shouldn't he? What reality could there be in comments upon American politics which ignored the colossal phenomenon of Roosevelt? If he is wholly evil, as many say he is, then the American democracy is preponderantly evil. For in the first years of the Twentieth Century, Roosevelt spoke for this nation, as few presidents have spoken in our history. And that he has spoken well, who in the perspective of time will deny? Sensitive to the original forces of public opinion, no man has had the same power of rounding up the laggards. Government under him was a throbbing human purpose. He succeeded, where Tart failed, in preventing that drought of invention which officialism brings. Many people say he has tried to be all things to all men—that his speeches are an attempt to corral all sorts of votes. That is a left-handed way of stating a truth. A more generous interpretation would be to say that he had tried to be inclusive, to attach a hundred sectional agitations to a national program. Crude: of course he was crude; he had a hemisphere for his canvas. Inconsistent: yes, he tried to be the leader of factions at war with one another. A late convert: he is a statesman and not an agitator—his business was to meet demands when they had grown to national proportions. No end of possibilities have slipped through the large meshes of his net. He has said some silly things. He has not been subtle, and he has been far from perfect. But his success should be judged by the size of his task, by the fierceness of the opposition, by the intellectual qualities of the nation he represented. When we remember that he was trained in the Republican politics of Hanna and Platt, that he was the first President who shared a new social vision, then I believe we need offer no apologies for making Mr. Roosevelt stand as the working model for a possible American statesman at the beginning of the Twentieth Century.

Critics have often suggested that Roosevelt stole Bryan's clothes. That is perhaps true, and it suggests a comparison which illuminates both men. It would not be unfair to say that it is always the function of the Roosevelts to take from the Bryans. But it is a little silly for an agitator to cry thief when the success of his agitation has led to the adoption of his ideas. It is like the chagrin of the socialists because the National Progressive Party had "stolen twenty-three planks," and it makes a person wonder whether some agitators haven't an overdeveloped sense of private property.

I do not see the statesman in Bryan. He has been something of a voice crying in the wilderness, but a voice that did not understand its own message. Many people talk of him as a prophet. There is a great deal of literal truth in that remark, for it has been the peculiar work of Bryan to express in politics some of that emotion which has made America the home of new religions. What we know as the scientific habit of mind is entirely lacking in his intellectual equipment. There is a vein of mysticism in American life, and Mr. Bryan is its uncritical prophet. His insights are those of the gifted evangelist, often profound and always narrow. It is absurd to debate his sincerity. Mr. Bryan talks with the intoxication of the man who has had a revelation: to skeptics that always seems theatrical. But far from being the scheming hypocrite his enemies say he is, Mr. Bryan is too simple for the task of statesmanship. No bracing critical atmosphere plays about his mind: there are no cleansing doubts and fruitful alternatives. The work of Bryan has been to express a certain feeling of unrest—to embody it in the traditional language of prophecy. But it is a shrewd turn of the American people that has kept him out of office. I say this not in disrespect of his qualities, but in definition of them. Bryan does not happen to have the naturalistic outlook, the complete humanity, or the deliberative habit which modern statecraft requires. He is the voice of a confused emotion.

Woodrow Wilson has a talent which is Bryan's chief defect—the scientific habit of holding facts in solution. His mind is lucid and flexible, and he has the faculty of taking advice quickly, of stating something he has borrowed with more ease and subtlety than the specialist from whom he got it. Woodrow Wilson's is an elegant and highly refined intellect, nicely balanced and capable of fine adjustment.

An urbane civilization produced it, leisure has given it spaciousness, ease has made it generous. A mind without tension, its roots are not in the somewhat barbarous under-currents of the nation. Woodrow Wilson understands easily, but he does not incarnate: he has never been a part of the protest he speaks. You think of him as a good counsellor, as an excellent presiding officer. Whether his imagination is fibrous enough to catch the inwardness of the mutterings of our age is something experience alone can show. Wilson has class feeling in the least offensive sense of that term: he likes a world of gentlemen. Occasionally he has exhibited a rather amateurish effort to be grimy and shirt-sleeved. But without much success: his contact with American life is not direct, and so he is capable of purely theoretical affirmations. Like all essentially contemplative men, the world has to be reflected in the medium of his intellect before he can grapple with it.

Yet Wilson belongs among the statesmen, and it is fine that he should be in public life. The weakness I have suggested is one that all statesmen share in some degree: an inability to interpret adequately the world they govern. This is a difficulty which is common to conservative and radical, and if I have used three living men to illustrate the problem it is only because they seem to illuminate it. They have faced the task and we can take their measurement. It is no part of my purpose to make any judgment as to the value of particular policies they have advocated. I am attempting to suggest some of the essentials of a statesman's equipment for the work of a humanly centered politics. Roosevelt has seemed to me the most effective, the most nearly complete;

Bryan I have ventured to class with the men who though important to politics should never hold high executive office; Wilson, less complete than Roosevelt, is worthy of our deepest interest because his judgment is subtle where Roosevelt's is crude. He is a foretaste of a more advanced statesmanship.

Because he is self-conscious, Wilson has been able to see the problem that any finely adapted statecraft must meet. It is a problem that would hardly occur to an old-fashioned politician: "Though he (the statesman) cannot himself keep the life of the nation as a whole in his mind, he can at least make sure that he is taking counsel with those who know. . . ." It is not important that Wilson in stating the difficulty should put it as if he had in a measure solved it. He hasn't, because taking counsel is a means to understanding the nation as a whole, and that understanding remains almost as arduous and requires just as fibrous an imagination, if it is gleaned from advisers.

To think of the whole nation: surely the task of statesmanship is more difficult to-day than ever before in history. In the face of a clotted intricacy in the subject-matter of politics, improvements in knowledge seem meager indeed. The distance between what we know and what we need to know appears to be greater than ever. Plato and Aristotle thought in terms of ten thousand homogeneous villagers; we have to think in terms of a hundred million people of all races and all traditions, crossbred and inbred, subject to climates they have never lived in before, plumped down on a continent in the midst of a strange civilization. We have to deal with all grades of life from the frontier to the metropolis, with men who differ in sense of fact, in ideal, in the very groundwork of morals. And we have to take into account not the simple opposition of two classes, but the hostility of many,—the farmers and the factory workers and all the castes within their ranks, the small merchants, and the feudal organization of business. Ours is a problem in which deception has become organized and strong; where truth is poisoned at its source; one in which the skill of the shrewdest brains is devoted to misleading a bewildered people. Nor can we keep to the problem within our borders. Whether we wish it or not we are involved in the world's problems, and all the winds of heaven blow through our land.

It is a great question whether our intellects can grasp the subject. Are we perhaps like a child whose hand is too small to span an octave on the piano? Not only are the facts inhumanly complicated, but the natural ideals of people are so varied and contradictory that action halts in despair. We are putting a tremendous strain upon the mind, and the results are all about us: everyone has known the neutral thinkers who stand forever undecided before the complications of life, who have, as it were, caught a glimpse of the possibilities of knowledge. The sight has paralyzed them. Unless they can act with certainty, they dare not act at all.

That is merely one of the temptations of theory. In the real world, action and thought are so closely related that one cannot wait upon the other. We cannot wait in politics for any completed theoretical discussion of its method: it is a monstrous demand. There is no pausing until political psychology is more certain. We have to act on what we believe, on half-knowledge, illusion and error. Experience itself will reveal our mistakes; research and criticism may convert them into wisdom. But act we must, and act as if we knew the nature of man and proposed to satisfy his needs.

In other words, we must put man at the center of politics, even though we are densely ignorant both of man and of politics. This has always been the method of great political thinkers from Plato to Bentham. But one difference we in this age must note: they made their political man a dogma— we must leave him an hypothesis. That is to say that our task is to temper speculation with scientific humility.

A paradox there is here, but a paradox of language, and not of fact. Men made bridges before there was a science of bridge-building; they cured disease before they knew medicine. Art came before aesthetics, and righteousness before ethics. Conduct and theory react upon each other. Hypothesis is confirmed and modified by action, and action is guided by hypothesis. If it is a paradox to ask for a human politics before we understand humanity or politics, it is what Mr. Chesterton describes as one of those paradoxes that sit beside the wells of truth.

We make our picture of man, knowing that, though it is crude and unjust, we have to work with it. If we are wise we shall become experimental towards life: then every mistake will contribute towards knowledge. Let the exploration of human need and desire become a deliberate purpose of statecraft, and there is no present measure of its possibilities.

In this work there are many guides. A vague common tradition is in the air about us—it expresses itself in journalism, in cheap novels, in the uncritical theater. Every merchant has his stock of assumptions about the mental habits of his customers and competitors; the prostitute hers; the newspaperman his; P. T. Barnum had a few; the vaudeville stage has a number. We test these notions by their results, and even "practical people" find that there is more variety in human nature than they had supposed.

We forge gradually our greatest instrument for understanding the world—introspection. We discover that humanity may resemble us very considerably—that the best way of knowing the inwardness of our neighbors is to know ourselves. For after all, the only experience we really understand is our own. And that, in the least of us, is so rich that no one has yet exhausted its possibilities. It has been said that every genuine character an artist produces is one of the characters he might have been. By re-creating our own suppressed possibilities we multiply the number of lives that we can really know. That as I understand it is the psychology of the Golden Rule. For note that Jesus did not set up some external fetich: he did not say, make your neighbor righteous, or chaste, or respectable. He said do as you would be done by. Assume that you and he are alike, and you can found morals on humanity.

But experience has enlarged our knowledge of differences. We realize now that our neighbor is not always like ourselves. Knowing how unjust other people's inferences are when they concern us, we have begun to guess that ours may be unjust to them. Any uniformity of conduct becomes at once an impossible ideal, and the willingness to live and let live assumes high place among the virtues. A puzzled wisdom remarks that "it takes all sorts of people to make a world," and half-protestingly men accept Bernard Shaw's amendment, "Do not do unto others as you would that they should do unto you. Their tastes may not be the same."

We learn perhaps that there is no contradiction in speaking of "human nature" while admitting that men are unique. For all deepening of our knowledge gives a greater sense of common likeness and individual variation. It is folly to ignore either insight. But it is done constantly, with no end of confusion as a result. Some men have got themselves into a state where the only view that interests them is the common humanity of us all. Their world is not populated by men and women, but by a Unity that is Permanent. You might as well refuse to see any differences between steam, water and ice because they have common elements. And I have seen some of these people trying to skate on steam. Their brothers, blind in the other eye, go about the world so sure that each person is entirely unique, that society becomes like a row of packing cases, each painted on the inside, and each containing one ego and its own.

Art enlarges experience by admitting us to the inner life of others. That is not the only use of art, for its function is surely greater and more ultimate than to furnish us with a better knowledge of human nature. Nor is that its only use even to statecraft. I suggested earlier that art enters politics as a "moral equivalent" for evil, a medium by which barbarous lusts find civilized expression. It is, too, an ideal for labor. But my purpose here is not to attempt any adequate description of the services of art. It is enough to note that literature in particular elaborates our insight into human life, and, therefore, enables us to center our institutions more truly.

Ibsen discovers a soul in Nora: the discovery is absorbed into the common knowledge of the age. Other Noras discover their own souls; the Helmers all about us begin to see the person in the doll. Plays and novels have indeed an overwhelming political importance, as the "moderns" have maintained. But it lies not in the preaching of a doctrine or the insistence on some particular change in conduct. That is a shallow and wasteful use of the resources of art. For art can open up the springs from which conduct flows. Its genuine influence is on what Wells calls the "hinterland," in a quickening of the sense of life.

Art can really penetrate where most of us can only observe. "I look and I think I see," writes Bergson, "I listen and I think I hear, I examine myself and I think I am reading the very depths of my heart. . . . (But) my senses and my consciousness . . . give me no more than a practical simplification of reality . . . in short, we do not see the actual things themselves; in most cases we confine ourselves to reading the labels affixed to them." Who has not known this in thinking of politics? We talk of poverty and forget poor people; we make rules for vagrancy—we forget the vagrant. Some of our best-intentioned political schemes, like reform colonies and scientific jails, turn out to be inhuman tyrannies just because our imagination does not penetrate the sociological label. "We move amidst generalities and symbols . . . we live in a zone midway between things and ourselves, external to things, external also to ourselves." This is what works of art help to correct: "Behind the commonplace, conventional expression that both reveals and conceals an individual mental state, it is the emotion, the original mood, to which they attain in its undefiled essence."

This directness of vision fertilizes thought. Without a strong artistic tradition, the life and so the politics of a nation sink into a barren routine. A country populated by pure logicians and mathematical scientists would, I believe, produce few inventions. For creation, even of scientific truth, is no automatic product of logical thought or scientific method, and it has been well said that the greatest discoveries in science are brilliant guesses on insufficient evidence. A nation must, so to speak, live close to its own life, be intimate and sympathetic with natural events. That is what gives understanding, and justifies the observation that the intuitions of scientific discovery and the artist's perceptions are closely related. It is perhaps not altogether without significance for us that primitive science and poetry were indistinguishable. Nor is it strange that latter-day research should confirm so many sayings of the poets. In all great ages art and science have enriched each other. It is only eccentric poets and narrow specialists who lock the doors. The human spirit doesn't grow in sections.

I shall not press the point for it would lead us far afield. It is enough that we remember the close alliance of art, science and politics in Athens, in Florence and Venice at their zenith. We in America have divorced them completely: both art and politics exist in a condition of unnatural celibacy. Is this not a contributing factor to the futility and opacity of our political thinking? We have handed over the government of a nation of people to a set of lawyers, to a class of men who deal in the most verbal and unreal of all human attainments.

A lively artistic tradition is essential to the humanizing of politics. It is the soil in which invention flourishes and the organized knowledge of science attains its greatest reality. Let me illustrate from another field of interests. The religious investigations of William James were a study, not of ecclesiastical institutions or the history of creeds. They were concerned with religious experience, of which churches and rituals are nothing but the external satisfaction. As Graham Wallas is endeavoring to make human nature the center of politics, so James made it the center of religions. It was a work of genius, yet no one would claim that it is a mature psychology of the "Varieties of Religious Experience." It is rather a survey and a description, done with the eye of an artist and the method of a scientist. We know from it more of what religious feeling is like, even though we remain ignorant of its sources. And this intimacy humanizes religious controversy and brings ecclesiasticism back to men.

Like most of James's psychology, it opens up investigation instead of concluding it. In the light even of our present knowledge we can see how primitive his treatment was. But James's services cannot be overestimated: if he did not lay even the foundations of a science, he did lay some of the foundations for research. It was an immense illumination and a warming of interest. It threw open the gates to the whole landscape of possibilities. It was a ventilation of thought. Something similar will have to be done for political psychology. We know how far off is the profound and precise knowledge we desire. But we know too that we have a right to hope for an increasing acquaintance with the varieties of political experience. It would, of course, be drawn from biography, from the human aspect of history and daily observation. We should begin to know what it is that we ought to know. Such a work would be stimulating to politician and psychologist. The statesman's imagination would be guided and organized; it would give him a starting-point for his own understanding of human beings in politics. To the scientists it would be a challenge—to bring these facts under the light of their researches, to extend these researches to the borders of those facts.

The statesman has another way of strengthening his grip upon the complexity of life. Statistics help. This method is neither so conclusive as the devotees say, nor so bad as the people who are awed by it would like to believe. Voting, as Gabriel Tarde points out, is our most conspicuous use of statistics. Mystical democrats believe that an election expresses the will of the people, and that that will is wise. Mystical democrats are rare. Looked at closely an election shows the quantitative division of the people on several alternatives. That choice is not necessarily wise, but it is wise to heed that choice. For it is a rough estimate of an important part of the community's sentiment, and no statecraft can succeed that violates it. It is often immensely suggestive of what a large number of people are in the future going to wish. Democracy, because it registers popular feeling, is at least trying to build truly, and is for that reason an enlightened form of government. So we who are democrats need not believe that the people are necessarily right in their choice: some of us are always in the minority, and not a little proud of the distinction. Voting does not extract wisdom from multitudes: its real value is to furnish wisdom about multitudes. Our faith in democracy has this very solid foundation: that no leader's wisdom can be applied unless the democracy comes to approve of it. To govern a democracy you have to educate it: that contact with great masses of men reciprocates by educating the leader. "The consent of the governed" is more than a safeguard against ignorant tyrants: it is an insurance against benevolent despots as well. In a rough way and with many exceptions, democracy compels law to approximate human need. It is a little difficult to see this when you live right in the midst of one. But in perspective there can be little question that of all governments democracy is the most relevant. Only humane laws can be successfully enforced; and they are the only ones really worth enforcing. Voting is a formal method of registering consent.

But all statistical devices are open to abuse and require constant correction. Bribery, false counting, disfranchisement are the cruder deceptions; they correspond to those enrolment statistics of a large university which are artificially fed by counting the same student several times if his courses happen to span two or three of the departments. Just as deceptive as plain fraud is the deceptive ballot. We all know how when the political tricksters were compelled to frame a direct primary law in New York they fixed the ballot so that it botched the election. Corporations have been known to do just that to their reports. Did not E. H. Harriman say of a well-known statistician that he could make an annual report tell any story you pleased? Still subtler is the seven-foot ballot of stupid, good intentions—the hyperdemocratic ballot in which you are asked to vote for the State Printer, and succeed only in voting under the party emblem.

Statistics then is no automatic device for measuring facts. You and I are forever at the mercy of the census-taker and the census-maker. That impertinent fellow who goes from house to house is one of the real masters of the statistical situation. The other is the man who organizes the results. For all the conclusions in the end rest upon their accuracy, honesty, energy and insight. Of course, in an obvious census like that of the number of people personal bias counts for so little that it is lost in the grand total. But the moment you begin inquiries into subjects which people prefer to conceal, the weakness of statistics becomes obvious. All figures which touch upon sexual subjects are nothing but the roughest guesses. No one would take a census of prostitution, illegitimacy, adultery, or venereal disease for a statement of reliable facts. There are religious statistics, but who that has traveled among men would regard the number of professing Christians as any index of the strength of Christianity, or the church attendance as a measure of devotion? In the supremely important subject of literacy, what classification yet devised can weigh the culture of masses of people? We say that such a percentage of the population cannot read or write. But the test of reading and writing is crude and clumsy. It is often administered by men who are themselves half-educated, and it is shot through with racial and class prejudice.

The statistical method is of use only to those who have found it out. This is achieved principally by absorbing into your thinking a lively doubt about all classifications and general terms, for they are the basis of statistical measurement. That done you are fairly proof against seduction. No better popular statement of this is to be found than H. G. Wells' little essay: "Skepticism of the Instrument." Wells has, of course, made no new discovery. The history of philosophy is crowded with quarrels as to how seriously we ought to take our classifications: a large part of the battle about Nominalism turns on this, the Empirical and Rational traditions divide on it; in our day the attacks of James, Bergson, and the "anti-intellectualists" are largely a continuation of this old struggle. Wells takes his stand very definitely with those who regard classification "as serviceable for the practical purposes of life" but nevertheless "a departure from the objective truth of things."

"Take the word chair," he writes. "When one says chair, one thinks vaguely of an average chair. But collect individual instances, think of armchairs and reading-chairs, and dining-room chairs and kitchen chairs, chairs that pass into benches, chairs that cross the boundary and become settees, dentists' chairs, thrones, opera stalls, seats of all sorts, those miraculous fungoid growths that cumber the floor of the Arts and Crafts Exhibition, and you will perceive what a lax bundle in fact is this simple straightforward term. In cooperation with an intelligent joiner I would undertake to defeat any definition of chair or chairishness that you gave me." Think then of the glib way in which we speak of "the unemployed," "the unfit," "the criminal," "the unemployable," and how easily we forget that behind these general terms are unique individials with personal histories and varying needs.

Even the most refined statistics are nothing but an abstraction. But if that truth is held clearly before the mind, the polygons and curves of the statisticians can be used as a skeleton to which the imagination and our general sense of life give some flesh and blood reality. Human statistics are illuminating to those who know humanity. I would not trust a hermit's inferences about the statistics of anything.

It is then no simple formula which answers our question. The problem of a human politics is not solved by a catch phrase. Criticism, of which these essays are a piece, can give the direction we must travel. But for the rest there is no smooth road built, no swift and sure conveyance at the door. We set out as if we knew; we act on the notions of man that we possess. Literature refines, science deepens, various devices extend it. Those who act on the knowledge at hand are the men of affairs. And all the while, research studies their results, artists express subtler perceptions, critics refine and adapt the general culture of the times. There is no other way but through this vast collaboration.

There is no short cut to civilization. We say that the truth will make us free. Yes, but that truth is a thousand truths which grow and change. Nor do I see a final state of blessedness. The world's end will surely find us still engaged in answering riddles. This changing focus in politics is a tendency at work all through our lives. There are many experiments. But the effort is half-conscious; only here and there does it rise to a deliberate purpose. To make it an avowed ideal—a thing of will and intelligence—is to hasten its coming, illumine its blunders, and, by giving it self-criticism, to convert mistakes into wisdom.

CHAPTER V

WELL MEANING
BUT UNMEANING
The Chicago Vice Report

I N casting about for a concrete example to illustrate some of the points under discussion I hesitated a long time before the wealth of material. No age has produced such a multitude of elaborate studies, and any selection was, of course, a limiting one. The Minority Report of the English Poor Law Commission has striking merits and defects, but for our purposes it inheres too deeply in British conditions. American tariff and trust investigations are massive enough in all conscience, but they are so partisan in their origin and so pathetically unattached to any recognized ideal of public policy that it seemed better to look elsewhere. Conservation had the virtue of arising out of a provident statesmanship, but its problems were largely technical.

The real choice narrowed itself finally to the Pittsburgh Survey and the Chicago Vice Report. Had I been looking for an example of the finest expert inquiry, there would have been little question that the vivid and intensive study of Pittsburgh's industrialism was the example to use. But I was looking for something more representative, and, therefore, more revealing. I did not want a detached study of some specially selected cross-section of what is after all not the typical economic life of America. The case demanded was one in which you could see representative American citizens trying to handle a problem which had touched their imaginations.

Vice is such a problem. You can always get a hearing about it; there is no end of interest in the question. Rare indeed is that community which has not been "Lexowed," in which a district attorney or a minister has not led a crusade. Muckraking began with the exposure of vice; men like Heney, Lindsey, Folk founded their reputations on the fight against it. It would be interesting to know how much of the social conscience of our time had as its first insight the prostitute on the city pavement.

We do not have to force an interest, as we do about the trusts, or even about the poor. For this problem lies close indeed to the dynamics of our own natures. Research is stimulated, actively aroused, and a passionate zeal suffuses what is perhaps the most spontaneous reform enthusiasm of our time. Looked at externally it is a curious focusing of attention. Nor is it explained by words like "chivalry," "conscience," "social compassion." Magazines that will condone a thousand cruelties to women gladly publish series of articles on the girl who goes wrong; merchants who sweat and rack their women employees serve gallantly on these commissions. These men are not conscious hypocrites. Perhaps like the rest of us they are impelled by forces they are not eager to examine. I do not press the point. It belongs to the analyst of motive.

Well Meaning But Unmeaning

We need only note the vast interest in the subject—that it extends across class lines, and expresses itself as an immense good-will. Perhaps a largely unconscious absorption in a subject is itself a sign of great importance. Surely vice has a thousand implications that touch all of us directly. It is closely related to most of the interests of life—ramifying into industry, into the family, health, play, art, religion. The miseries it entails are genuine miseries—not points of etiquette or infringements of convention. Vice issues in pain. The world suffers for it. To attack it is to attack as far-reaching and real a problem as any that we human beings face.

The Chicago Commission had no simple, easily measured problem before it. At the very outset the report confesses that an accurate count of the number of prostitutes in Chicago could not be reached. The police lists are obviously incomplete and perhaps corrupt. The whole amorphous field of clandestine vice will, of course, defeat any census. But even public prostitution is so varied that nobody can do better than estimate it roughly. This point is worth keeping in mind, for it lights up the remedies proposed. What the Commission advocates is the constant repression and the ultimate annihilation of a mode of life which refuses discovery and measurement.

The report estimates that there are five thousand women in Chicago who devote their whole time to the traffic; that the annual profits in that one city alone are between fifteen and sixteen million dollars a year. These figures are admittedly low for they leave out all consideration of occasional, or seasonal, or hidden prostitution. It is only the nucleus that can be guessed at; the fringe which shades out into various degrees of respectability remains entirely un-measured. Yet these suburbs of the Tenderloin must always be kept in mind; their population is shifting and very elastic; it includes the unsuspected; and I am inclined to believe that it is the natural refuge of the "suppressed" prostitute. More-over it defies control.

The 1012 women recognized on the police lists are of course the most easily studied. From them we can gather some hint of the enormous bewildering demand that prosti-tution answers. The Commission informs us that this small group alone receives over fifteen thousand visits a day—five million and a half in the year. Yet these 1012 women are only about one-fifth of the professional prostitutes in Chicago. If the average continues, then the figures mount to something over 27,000,000. The five thousand profes-sionals do not begin to represent the whole illicit traffic of a city like Chicago. Clandestine and occasional vice is beyond all measurement.

The figures I have given are taken from the report. They are said to be conservative. For the purposes of this discus-sion we could well lower the 27,000,000 by half. All I am concerned about is in arriving at a sense of the enormity of the impulse behind the "social evil." For it is this that the Commission proposes to repress, and ultimately to annihilate.

Lust has a thousand avenues. The brothel, the flat, the assignation house, the tenement, saloons, dance halls, steamers, ice-cream parlors, Turkish baths, massage parlors, street-walking—the thing has woven itself into the texture of city life. Like the hydra, it grows new heads, everywhere. It draws into its service the pleasures of the city. Entangled with the love of gaiety, organized as commerce, it is literally impossible to follow the myriad expressions it assumes.

The Commission gives a very fair picture of these manifestations. A mass of material is offered which does in a way show where and how and to what extent lust finds its illicit expression. Deeper than this the report does not go. The human impulses which create these social conditions, the human needs to which they are a sad and degraded answer—this human center of the problem the commission passes by with a platitude.

"So long as there is lust in the hearts of men," we are told, "it will seek out some method of expression. Until the hearts of men are changed we can hope for no absolute annihilation of the Social Evil." But at the head of the report in black-faced type we read: "Constant and persistent repression of prostitution the immediate method; absolute annihilation the ultimate ideal."

I am not trying to catch the Commissioners in a verbal inconsistency. The inconsistency is real, out of a deep-seated confusion of mind. Lust will seek an expression, they say, until "the hearts of men are changed." All particular expressions are evil and must be constantly repressed. Yet though you repress one form of lust, it will seek some other. Now, says the Commission, in order to change the hearts of men, religion and education must step in. It is their business to eradicate an impulse which is constantly changing form by being "suppressed."

There is only one meaning in this: the Commission realized vaguely that repression is not even the first step to a cure. For reasons worth analyzing later, these representative

American citizens desired both the immediate taboo and an ultimate annihilation of vice. So they fell into the confusion of making immediate and detailed proposals that have nothing to do with the attainment of their ideal.

What the commission saw and described were the particular forms which a great human impulse had assumed at a specific date in a certain city. The dynamic force which created these conditions, which will continue to create them—lust—they refer to in a few pious sentences. Their thinking, in short, is perfectly static and literally superficial. In outlining a ripple they have forgotten the tides.

Had they faced the human sources of their problem, had they tried to think of the social evil as an answer to a human need, their researches would have been different, their remedies fruitful. Suppose they had kept in mind their own statement: "so long as there is lust in the hearts of men it will seek out some method of expression." Had they held fast to that, it would have ceased to be a platitude and have become a fertile idea. For a platitude is generally inert wisdom.

In the sentence I quote the Commissioners had an idea which might have animated all their labors. But they left it in limbo, they reverenced it, and they passed by. Perhaps we can raise it again and follow the hints it unfolds.

If lust will seek an expression, are all expressions of it necessarily evil? That the kind of expression which the Commission describes is evil no one will deny. But is it the only possible expression?

If it is, then the taboo enforced by a Morals Police is, perhaps, as good a way as any of gaining a fictitious sense of activity. But the ideal of "annihilation" becomes an irrelevant and meaningless phrase. If lust is deeply rooted in men and its only expression is evil, I for one should recommend a faith in the millennium. You can put this Paradise at the beginning of the world or the end of it. Practical difference there is none.

No one can read the report without coming to a definite conviction that the Commission regards lust itself as inherently evil. The members assumed without criticism the traditional dogma of Christianity that sex in any manifestation outside of marriage is sinful. But practical sense told them that sex cannot be confined within marriage. It will find expression—"some method of expression" they say. What never occurred to them was that it might find a good, a positively beneficent method. The utterly uncriticised assumption that all expressions not legalized are sinful shut them off from any constructive answer to their problem. Seeing prostitution or something equally bad as the only way sex can find an expression they really set before religion and education the impossible task of removing lust "from the hearts of men." So when their report puts at its head that absolute annihilation of prostitution is the ultimate ideal, we may well translate it into the real intent of the Commission. What is to be absolutely annihilated is not alone prostitution, not alone all the methods of expression which lust seeks out, but lust itself.

That this is what the Commission had in mind is supported by plenty of "internal evidence." For example: one of the most curious recommendations made is about divorce—"The Commission condemns the ease with which divorces may be obtained in certain States, and recommends a stringent, uniform divorce law for all States."

What did the Commission have in mind? I transcribe the paragraph which deals with divorce: "The Vice Commission, after exhaustive consideration of the vice question, records itself of the opinion that divorce to a large extent is a contributory factor to sexual vice. No study of this blight upon the social and moral life of the country would be comprehensive without consideration of the causes which lead to the application for divorce. These are too numerous to mention at length in such a report as this, but the Commission does wish to emphasize the great need of more safeguards against the marrying of persons physically, mentally and morally unfit to take up the responsibilities of family life, including the bearing of children."

Now to be sure that paragraph leaves much to be desired so far as clearness goes. But I think the meaning can be extracted. Divorce is a contributory factor to sexual vice. One way presumably is that divorced women often become prostitutes. That is an evil contribution, unquestionably. The second sentence says that no study of the social evil is complete which leaves out the *causes* of divorce. One of those causes is, I suppose, adultery with a prostitute. This evil is totally different from the first: in one case divorce contributes to prostitution, in the other, prostitution leads to divorce. The third sentence urges greater safeguards against undesirable marriages. This prudence would obviously reduce the need of divorce.

How does the recommendation of a stringent and uniform law fit in with these three statements? A strict divorce law might be like New York's: it would recognize few grounds for a decree. One of those grounds, perhaps the chief one, would be adultery. I say this unhesitatingly for in another place the Commission informs us that marriage has in it "the elements of vested rights."

A strict divorce law would, of course, diminish the number of "divorced women," and perhaps keep them out of prostitution. It does fit the first statement—in a helpless sort of way. But where does the difficulty of divorce affect the causes of it? If you bind a man tightly to a woman he does not love, and, possibly prevent him from marrying one he does love, how do you add to his virtue? And if the only way he can free himself is by adultery, does not your stringent divorce law put a premium upon vice? The third sentence would make it difficult for the unfit to marry. Better marriages would among other blessings require fewer divorces. But what of those who are forbidden to marry? They are unprovided for. And yet who more than they are likely to find desire uncontrollable and seek some other "method of expression"? With marriage prohibited and prostitution tabooed, the Commission has a choice between sterilization and—let us say—other methods of expression.

Make marriage difficult, divorce stringent, prostitution impossible—is there any doubt that the leading idea is to confine the sex impulse within the marriage of healthy, intelligent, "moral," and monogamous couples? For all the other seekings of that impulse what has the Commission to offer? Nothing. That can be asserted flatly. The Commission hopes to wipe out prostitution. But it never hints that the success of its plan means vast alterations in our social life. The members give the impression that they think of prostitution as something that can be subtracted from our civilization without changing the essential character of its institutions. Yet who that has read the report itself and put himself into any imaginative understanding of conditions can escape seeing that prostitution to-day is organic to our industrial life, our marriage sanctions, and our social customs? Low wages, fatigue, and the wretched monotony of the factory—these must go before prostitution can go. And behind these stand the facts of woman's entrance into industry—facts that have one source at least in the general poverty of the family. And that poverty is deeply bound up with the economic system under which we live. In the man's problem, the growing impossibility of early marriages is directly related to the business situation. Nor can we speak of the degradation of religion and the arts, of amusement, of the general morale of the people without referring that degradation to industrial conditions.

You cannot look at civilization as a row of institutions each external to the other. They interpenetrate and a change in one affects all the others. To abolish prostitution would involve a radical alteration of society. Vice in our cities is a form of the sexual impulse—one of the forms it has taken under prevailing social conditions. It is, if you please, like the crops of a rude and forbidding soil—a coarse, distorted thing though living.

The Commission studied a human problem and left humanity out. I do not mean that the members weren't deeply touched by the misery of these thousands of women. You can pity the poor without understanding them; you can have compassion without insight. The Commissioners had a good deal of sympathy for the prostitute's condition, but for that "lust in the hearts of men," and women we may add, for that, they had no sympathetic understanding. They did not place themselves within the impulse. Officially they remained external to human desires. For what might be called the *élan vital* of the problem they had no patience. Certain sad results of the particular "method of expression" it had sought out in Chicago called forth their pity and their horror.

In short, the Commission did not face the sexual impulse squarely. The report is an attempt to deal with a sexual problem by disregarding its source. There are almost a hundred recommendations to various authorities—Federal, State, county, city, police, educational and others. I have attempted to classify these proposals under four headings. There are those which mean forcible repression of particular manifestations—the taboos; there are the recommendations which are purely palliative, which aim to abate some of the horrors of existing conditions; there are a few suggestions for further investigation; and, finally, there are the inventions, the plans which show some desire to find moral equivalents for evil—the really statesmanlike offerings.

The palliative measures we may pass by quickly. So long as they do not blind people to the necessity for radical treatment, only a doctrinaire would object to them. Like all intelligent charities they are still a necessary evil. But nothing must be staked upon them, so let us turn at once to the constructive suggestions: The Commission proposes that the county establish a "Permanent Committee on Child Protection." It makes no attempt to say what that protection shall be, but I think it is only fair to let the wish father the thought, and regard this as an effort to give children a better start in life. The separation of delinquent from semi-delinquent girls is a somewhat similar attempt to guard the weak. Another is the recommendation to the city and the nation that it should protect arriving immigrants, and if necessary escort them to their homes. This surely is a constructive plan which might well be enlarged from mere protection to positive hospitality. How great a part the desolating loneliness of a city plays in seductions the individual histories in the report show. Municipal dance halls are a splendid proposal. Freed from a cold and over-chaperoned respectability they compete with the devil. There, at least, is one method of sexual expression which may have positively beneficent results. A municipal lodging house for women is something of a substitute for the wretched rented room. A little suggestion to the police that they send home children found on the streets after nine o'clock has varied possibilities. But there is the seed of an invention in it which might convert the police from mere agents of repression to kindly helpers in the mazes of a city. The educational proposals are all constructive: the teaching of sex hygiene is guardedly recommended for consideration. That is entirely justified, for no one can quarrel with a set of men for leaving a question open. That girls from fourteen to sixteen should receive vocational training in continuation schools; that social centers should be established in the public schools and that the grounds should be open for children—all of these are clearly additions to the positive resource of the community. So is the suggestion that church buildings be used for recreation. The call for greater parental responsibility is, I fear, a rather empty platitude, for it is not re-enforced with anything but an ancient fervor.

How much of this really seeks to create a fine expression of the sexual impulse? How many of these recommendations see sex as an instinct which can be transmuted, and turned into one of the values of life? The dance halls, the social centers, the playgrounds, the reception of strangers—these can become instruments for civilizing sexual need. The educational proposals could become ways of directing it. They could, but will they? Without the habit of mind which sees substitution as the essence of statecraft, without a philosophy which makes the invention of moral equivalents its goal, I for one refuse to see in these recommendations anything more than a haphazard shooting which has accidentally hit the mark. Moreover, I have a deep suspicion that I have tried to read into the proposals more than the Commission intended. Certainly these constructions occupy an insignificant amount of space in the body of the report. On all sides of them is a mass of taboos. No emotional appeal is made for them as there is for the repressions. They stand largely unnoticed, and very much undefined—poor ghosts of the truth among the gibbets.

An inadvertent platitude—that lust will seek an expression—and a few diffident proposals for a finer environment—the need and its satisfaction: had the Commission seen the relation of these incipient ideas, animated it, and made it the nerve center of the study, a genuine program might have resulted. But the two ideas never met and fertilized each other. Nothing dynamic holds the recommendations together—the mass of them are taboos, an attempt to kill each mosquito and ignore the marsh. The evils of prostitution are seen as a series of episodes, each of which must be clubbed, forbidden, raided and jailed.

There is a special whack for each mosquito: the laws about excursion boats should be enforced; the owners should help to enforce them; there should be more officers with police power on these boats; the sale of liquor to minors should be forbidden; gambling devices should be suppressed; the midwives, doctors and maternity hospitals practicing abortions should be investigated; employment agencies should be watched and investigated; publishers should be warned against printing suspicious advertisements; the law against infamous crimes should be made more specific; any citizen should have the right to bring equity proceedings against a brothel as a public nuisance; there should be relentless prosecution of professional procurers; there should be constant prosecution of the keepers, inmates, and owners of bawdy houses; there should be prosecution of druggists who sells drugs and "certain appliances" illegally; there should be an identification system for prostitutes in the state courts; instead of fines, prostitutes should be visited with imprisonment or adult probation; there should be a penalty for sending messenger boys under twenty-one to a disorderly house or an unlicensed saloon; the law against prostitutes in saloons, against wine-rooms and stalls in saloons, against communication between saloons and brothels, against dancing in saloons—should be strictly enforced; the police who enforce these laws should be carefully watched, grafters amongst them should be discharged; complaints should be investigated at once by a man stationed outside the district; the pressure of publicity should be brought against the brewers to prevent them from doing business with saloons that violate the law; the Retail Liquor Association should discipline law-breaking saloon-keepers: licenses should be permanently revoked for violations; no women should be allowed in a saloon without a male escort; no professional or paid escorts should be permitted; no soliciting should be allowed in saloons; no immoral or vulgar dances should be permitted in saloons; no intoxicating liquor should be allowed at any public dance; there should be a municipal detention home for women, with probation officers; police inspectors who fail to report law-violations should be dismissed; assignation houses should be suppressed as soon as they are reported; there should be a "special morals police squad"; recommendation IX "to the Police" says they "should wage a relentless warfare against houses of prostitution, immoral flats, assignation rooms, call houses, and disorderly saloons in all sections of the city"; parks and playgrounds should be more thoroughly policed; dancing pavilions should exclude professional prostitutes; soliciting in parks should be suppressed; parks should be lighted with a search-light; there should be no seats in the shadows. . . .

To perform that staggering list of things that "should" be done you find—what?—the police power, federal, state, municipal. Note how vague and general are the chance constructive suggestions; how precise and definite the taboos. Surely I am not misstating its position when I say that forcible suppression was the creed of this Commission. Nor is there any need of insisting again that the ultimate ideal of annihilating prostitution has nothing to expect from the concrete proposals that were made. The millennial goal was one thing; the immediate method quite another. For ideals, a pious phrase; in practice, the police.

Are we not told that "if the citizens cannot depend upon the men appointed to protect their property, and to maintain order, then chaos and disorganization resulting in vice and crime must follow?" Yet of all the reeds that civilization leans upon, surely the police is the frailest. Anyone who has had the smallest experience of municipal politics knows that the corruption of the police is directly proportionate to the severity of the taboos it is asked to enforce. Tom Johnson saw this as Mayor of Cleveland; he knew that strict law enforcement against saloons, brothels, and gambling houses would not stop vice, but would corrupt the police. I recommend the recent spectacle in New York where the most sensational raider of gambling houses has turned out to be in crooked alliance with the gamblers. And I suggest as a hint that the Commission's recommendations enforced for one year will lay the foundation of an organized system of blackmail and "protection," secrecy and underground chicanery, the like of which Chicago has not yet seen. But the Commission need only have read its own report, have studied its own cases. There is an illuminating chapter on "The Social Evil and the Police." In the summary, the Commission says that "officers on the beat are bold and open in their neglect of duty, drinking in saloons while in uniform, ignoring the solicitations by prostitutes in rear rooms and on the streets, selling tickets at dances frequented by professional and semi-professional prostitutes; protecting 'cadets,' prostitutes and saloon-keepers of disorderly places."

Some suspicion that the police could not carry the burden of suppressing the social evil must have dawned on the Commission.

It felt the need of re-enforcement. Hence the special morals police squad; hence the investigation of the police of one district by the police from another; and hence, in type as black as that of the ideal itself and directly beneath it, the call for "the appointment of a morals commission" and "the establishment of a morals court." Now this commission consists of the Health Officer, a physician and three citizens who serve without pay. It is appointed by the Mayor and approved by the City Council. Its business is to prosecute vice and to help enforce the law.

Just what would happen if the Morals Commission didn't prosecute hard enough I do not know. Conceivably the Governor might be induced to appoint a Commission on Moral Commissions in Cities. But why the men and women who framed the report made this particular recommendation is an interesting question. With federal, state, and municipal authorities in existence, with courts, district attorneys, police all operating, they create another arm of prosecution. Possibly they were somewhat disillusioned about the present instruments of the taboo; perhaps they imagined that a new broom would sweep clean. But I suspect an inner reason. The Commission may have imagined that the four appointees—unpaid—would be four men like themselves—who knows, perhaps four men from among themselves? The whole tenor of their thinking is to set somebody watching everybody and somebody else to watching him. What is more natural than that they should be the Ultimate Watchers?

Spying, informing, constant investigations of everybody and everything must become the rule where there is a forcible attempt to moralize society from the top. Nobody's heart is in the work very long; nobody's but those fanatical and morbid guardians of morality who make it a life's specialty. The aroused public opinion which the Commission asks for cannot be held if all it has to fix upon is an elaborate series of taboos. Sensational disclosures will often make the public flare up spasmodically; but the mass of men is soon bored by intricate rules and tangles of red tape; the "crusade" is looked upon as a melodrama of real life—interesting, but easily forgotten.

The method proposed ignores the human source: by a kind of poetic justice the great crowd of men will ignore the method. If you want to impose a taboo upon a whole community, you must do it autocratically, you must make it part of the prevailing superstitions. You must never let it reach any public analysis. For it will fail, it will receive only a shallow support from what we call an "enlightened public opinion." That opinion is largely determined by the real impulses of men; and genuine character rejects or at least rebels against foreign, unnatural impositions. This is one of the great virtues of democracy—that it makes alien laws more and more difficult to enforce. The tyrant can use the taboo a thousand times more effectively than the citizens of a republic. When he speaks, it is with a prestige that dumbs questioning and makes obedience a habit. Let that infallibility come to be doubted, as in Russia to-day, and natural impulses reassert themselves, the great impositions begin to weaken. The methods of the Chicago Commission would require a tyranny, a powerful, centralized sovereignty which could command with majesty and silence the rebel. In our shirt-sleeved republic no such power exists. The strongest force we have is that of organized money, and that sovereignty is too closely connected with the social evil, too dependent upon it in a hundred different ways, to undertake the task of suppression.

For the purposes of the Commission democracy is an inefficient weapon. Nothing but disappointment is in store for men who expect a people to outrage its own character. A large part of the unfaith in democracy, of the desire to ignore "the mob," limit the franchise, and confine power to the few is the result of an unsuccessful attempt to make republics act like old-fashioned monarchies. Almost every "crusade" leaves behind it a trail of yearning royalists; many "good-government" clubs are little would-be oligarchies.

When the mass of men emerged from slavish obedience and made democracy inevitable, the taboo entered upon its final illness. For the more self-governing a people becomes, the less possible it is to prescribe external restrictions. The gap between want and ought, between nature and ideals cannot be maintained. The only practical ideals in a democracy are a fine expression of natural wants. This happens to be a thoroughly Greek attitude. But I learned it first from the Bowery. Chuck Connors is reported to have said that "a gentleman is a bloke as can do whatever he wants to do." If Chuck said that, he went straight to the heart of that democratic morality on which a new statecraft must ultimately rest. His gentleman is not the battlefield of wants and prohibitions; in him impulses flow freely through beneficent channels.

The same notion lies imbedded in the phrase: "government must serve the people." That means a good deal more than that elected officials must rule for the majority. For the majority in these semi-democratic times is often as not a cloak for the ruling oligarchy. Representatives who "serve" some majorities may in reality order the nation about. To serve the people means to provide it with services—with clean streets and water, with education, with opportunity, with beneficent channels for its desires, with moral equivalents for evil. The task is turned from the damming and restricting of wants to the creation of fine environments for them. And the environment of an impulse extends all the way from the human body, through family life and education out into the streets of the city.

Had the Commission worked along democratic lines, we should have had recommendations about the hygiene and early training of children, their education, the houses they live in and the streets in which they play; changes would have been suggested in the industrial conditions they face; plans would have been drawn for recreation; hints would have been collected for transmuting the sex impulse into art, into social endeavor, into religion. That is the constructive approach to the problem. I note that the Commission calls upon the churches for help. Its obvious intention was to down sex with religion. What was not realized, it seems, is that this very sex impulse, so largely degraded into vice, is the dynamic force in religious feeling. One need not call in the testimony of the psychologists, the students of religion, the aestheticians or even of Plato, who in the "Symposium" traced out the hierarchy of love from the body to the "whole sea of beauty." Jane Addams in Chicago has tested the truth by her own wide experience, and she has written what the Commission might easily have read,—that "in failing to diffuse and utilize this fundamental instinct of sex through the imagination, we not only inadvertently foster vice and enervation, but we throw away one of the most precious implements for ministering to life's highest needs. There is no doubt that this ill-adjusted function consumes quite unnecessarily vast stores of vital energy, even when we contemplate it in its immature manifestations which are infinitely more wholesome than the dumb swamping process. All high school boys and girls know the difference between the concentration and the diffusion of this impulse, although they would be hopelessly bewildered by the use of terms. They will declare one of their companions to be 'in love' if his fancy is occupied by the image of a single person about whom all the new-found values gather, and without whom his solitude is an eternal melancholy. But if the stimulus does not appear as a definite image, and the values evoked are dispensed over the world, the young person suddenly seems to have discovered a beauty and significance in many things—he responds to poetry, he becomes a lover of nature, he is filled with religious devotion or with philanthropic zeal. Experience, with young people, easily illustrates the possibility and value of diffusion."

It is then not only impossible to confine sex to mere reproduction; it would be a stupid denial of the finest values

[*127*]

of civilization. Having seen that the impulse is a necessary part of character, we must not hold to it grudgingly as a necessary evil. It is, on the contrary, the very source of good. Whoever has visited Hull House can see for himself the earnest effort Miss Addams has made to treat sex with dignity and joy. For Hull House differs from most settlements in that it is full of pictures, of color, and of curios. The atmosphere is light; you feel none of that moral oppression which hangs over the usual settlement as over a gathering of missionaries. Miss Addams has not only made Hull House a beautiful place; she has stocked it with curious and interesting objects. The theater, the museum, the crafts and the arts, games and dances—they are some of those "other methods of expression which lust can seek." It is no accident that Hull House is the most successful settlement in America.

Yet who does not feel its isolation in that brutal city? A little Athens in a vast barbarism—you wonder how much of Chicago Hull House can civilize. As you walk those grim streets and look into the stifling houses, or picture the relentless stockyards, the conviction that vice and its misery cannot be transmuted by policemen and Morals Commissions, the feeling that spying and inspecting and prosecuting will not drain the marsh becomes a certainty. You want to shout at the forcible moralizer: "so long as you acquiesce in the degradation of your city, so long as work remains nothing but ill-paid drudgery and every instinct of joy is mocked by dirt and cheapness and brutality,—just so long will your efforts be fruitless, yes even though you raid and prosecute, even though you make Comstock the Czar of Chicago."

Well Meaning But Unmeaning

But Hull House cannot remake Chicago. A few hundred lives can be changed, and for the rest it is a guide to the imagination. Like all utopias, it cannot succeed, but it may point the way to success. If Hull House is unable to civilize Chicago, it at least shows Chicago and America what a civilization might be like. Friendly, where our cities are friendless, beautiful, where they are ugly; sociable and open, where our daily life is furtive; work a craft; art a participation—it is in miniature the goal of statesmanship. If Chicago were like Hull House, we say to ourselves, then vice would be no problem—it would dwindle, what was left would be the Falstaff in us all, and only a spiritual anemia could worry over that jolly and redeeming coarseness.

What stands between Chicago and civilization? No one can doubt that to abolish prostitution means to abolish the slum and the dirty alley, to stop overwork, underpay, the sweating and the torturing monotony of business, to breathe a new life into education, ventilate society with frankness, and fill life with play and art, with games, with passions which hold and suffuse the imagination.

It is a revolutionary task, and like all real revolutions it will not be done in a day or a decade because someone orders it to be done. A change in the whole quality of life is something that neither the policeman's club nor an insurrectionary raid can achieve. If you want a revolution that shall really matter in human life—and what sane man can help desiring it?—you must look to the infinitely complicated results of the dynamic movements in society. These revolutions require a rare combination of personal audacity and social patience. The best agents of such a revolution are men who are bold in their plans because they realize how deep and enormous is the task.

Many people have sought an analogy in our Civil War. They have said that as "black slavery" went, so must "white slavery." In the various agitations of vigilance committees and alliances for the suppression of the traffic they profess to see continued a work which the abolitionists began.

In A. M. Simons' brilliant book on "Social Forces in American History" much help can be found. For example: "Massachusetts abolished slavery at an early date, and we have it on the authority of John Adams that:—'argument might have had some weight in the abolition of slavery in Massachusetts, but the real cause was the multiplication of laboring white people, who would not longer suffer the rich to employ these sable rivals so much to their injury.'" No one to-day doubts that white labor in the North and slavery in the South were not due to the moral superiority of the North. Yet just in the North we find the abolition sentiment strongest. That the Civil War was not a clash of good men and bad men is admitted by every reputable historian. The war did not come when moral fervor had risen to the exploding point; the moral fervor came rather when the economic interests of the South collided with those of the North. That the abolitionists clarified the economic interests of the North and gave them an ideal sanction is true enough. But the fact remains that by 1860 some of the aspirations of Phillips and Garrison had become the economic destiny of this country.

You can have a Hull House established by private initiative and maintained by individual genius, just as you had planters who freed their slaves or as you have employers to-day who humanize their factories. But the fine example is not readily imitated when industrial forces fight against it. So even if the Commission had drawn splendid plans for housing, work conditions, education, and play it would have done only part of the task of statesmanship. We should then know what to do, but not how to get it done.

An ideal suspended in a vacuum is ineffective: it must point a dynamic current. Only then does it gather power, only then does it enter into life. That forces exist to-day which carry with them solutions is evident to anyone who has watched the labor movement and the woman's awakening. Even the interests of business give power to the cause. The discovery of manufacturers that degradation spoils industrial efficiency must not be cast aside by the radical because the motive is larger profits. The discovery, whatever the motive, will inevitably humanize industry a good deal. For it happens that in this case the interests of capitalism and of humanity coincide. A propaganda like the single-tax will undoubtedly find increasing support among business men. They see in it a relief from the burden of rent imposed by that older tyrant—the landlord. But the taxation of unimproved property happens at the same time to be a splendid weapon against the slum.

Only when the abolition of "white slavery" becomes part of the social currents of the time will it bear any interesting analogy to the so-called freeing of the slaves. Even then for many enthusiasts the comparison is misleading. They are likely to regard the Emancipation Proclamation as the end of chattel slavery. It wasn't. That historic document broke a legal bond but not a social one. The process of negro emancipation is infinitely slower and it is not accomplished yet. Likewise no statute can end "white slavery." Only vast and complicated changes in the whole texture of social life will achieve such an end. If by some magic every taboo of the commission could be enforced the abolition of sex slavery would not have come one step nearer to reality. Cities and factories, schools and homes, theaters and games, manners and thought will have to be transformed before sex can find a better expression. Living forces, not statutes or clubs, must work that change. The power of emancipation is in the social movements which alone can effect any deep reform in a nation. So it is and has been with the negro. I do not think the Abolitionists saw facts truly when they disbanded their organization a few years after the civil war. They found too much comfort in a change of legal status. Profound economic forces brought about the beginning of the end of chattel slavery. But the reality of freedom was not achieved by proclamation. For that the revolution had to go on: the industrial life of the nation had to change its character, social customs had to be replaced, the whole outlook of men had to be transformed. And whether it is negro slavery or a vicious sexual bondage, the actual advance comes from substitutions injected into society by dynamic social forces.

I do not wish to press the analogy or over-emphasize the particular problems. I am not engaged in drawing up the plans for a reconstruction or in telling just what should be done. Only the co-operation of expert minds can do that. The place for a special propaganda is elsewhere. If these essays succeed in suggesting a method of looking at politics, if they draw attention to what is real in social reforms and make somewhat more evident the traps and the blind-alleys of an uncritical approach, they will have done their work. That the report of the Chicago Vice Commission figures so prominently in this chapter is not due to any preoccupation with Chicago, the Commission or with vice. It is a text and nothing else. The report happens to embody what I conceive to be most of the faults of a political method now decadent. Its failure to put human impulses at the center of thought produced remedies valueless to human nature; its false interest in a particular expression of sex—vice—caused it to taboo the civilizing power of sex; its inability to see that wants require fine satisfactions and not prohibitions drove it into an undemocratic tyranny; its blindness to the social forces of our age shut off the motive power for any reform.

The Commission's method was poor, not its intentions. It was an average body of American citizens aroused to action by an obvious evil. But something slipped in to falsify vision. It was, I believe, an array of idols disguised as ideals. They are typical American idols, and they deserve some study.

Chapter VI

Some Necessary Iconoclasm

The Commission "has kept constantly in mind that to offer a contribution of any value such an offering must be, first, moral; second, reasonable and practical; third, possible under the Constitutional powers of our Courts; fourth, that which will square with the public conscience of the American people."

—The Vice Commission of Chicago
Introduction to Report on the Social Evil.

HAVING adjusted such spectacles the Commission proceeded to look at "this curse which is more blasting than any plague or epidemic," at an evil "which spells only ruin to the race." In dealing with what it regards as the greatest calamity in the world, a calamity as old as civilization, the Commission lays it down beforehand that the remedy must be "moral," constitutional, and satisfactory to the public conscience. I wonder in all seriousness what the Commission would have done had it discovered a genuine cure for prostitution which happened, let us say, to conflict with the constitutional powers of our courts. I wonder

how the Commission would have acted if a humble following of the facts had led them to a conviction out of tune
with the existing public conscience of America. Such a conflict is not only possible; it is highly probable. When you
come to think of it, the conflict appears a certainty. For the
Constitution is a legal expression of the conditions under
which prostitution has flourished; the social evil is rooted in
institutions and manners which have promoted it, in property relations and business practice which have gathered
about them a halo of reason and practicality, of morality and
conscience. Any change so vast as the abolition of vice is of
necessity a change in morals, practice, law and conscience.

A scientist who began an investigation by saying that his
results must be moral or constitutional would be a joke. We
have had scientists like that, men who insisted that research
must confirm the Biblical theory of creation. We have had
economists who set out with the preconceived idea of justifying the factory system. The world has recently begun to
see through this kind of intellectual fraud. If a doctor should
appear who offered a cure for tuberculosis on the ground that
it was justified by the Bible and that it conformed to the
opinions of that great mass of the American people who
believe that fresh air is the devil, we should promptly lock
up that doctor as a dangerous quack. When the negroes of
Kansas were said to be taking pink pills to guard themselves
against Halley's Comet, they were doing something which
appeared to them as eminently practical and entirely reasonable. Not long ago we read of the savage way in which a
leper was treated out West; his leprosy was not regarded as
a disease, but as the curse of God, and, if I remember cor-

rectly, the Bible was quoted in court as an authority on leprosy. The treatment seemed entirely moral and squared very well with the conscience of that community.

I have heard reputable physicians condemn a certain method of psychotherapy because it was "immoral." A woman once told me that she had let her son grow up ignorant of his sexual life because "a mother should never mention anything 'embarrassing' to her child." Many of us are still blushing for the way America treated Gorki when it found that Russian morals did not square with the public conscience of America. And the time is not yet passed when we punish the offspring of illicit love, and visit vengeance unto the third and fourth generations. One reads in the report of the Vice Commission that many public hospitals in Chicago refuse to care for venereal diseases. The examples are endless. They run from the absurd to the monstrous. But always the source is the same. Idols are set up to which all the living must bow; we decide beforehand that things must fit a few preconceived ideas. And when they don't, which is most of the time, we deny truth, falsify facts, and prefer the coddling of our theory to any deeper understanding of the real problem before us.

It seems as if a theory were never so active as when the reality behind it has disappeared. The empty name, the ghostly phrase, exercise an authority that is appalling. When you think of the blood that has been shed in the name of Jesus, when you think of the Holy Roman Empire, "neither holy nor Roman nor imperial," of the constitutional phrases that cloak all sorts of thievery, of the common law precedents that tyrannize over us, history begins to look almost like the struggle of man to emancipate himself from phrase-worship. The devil can quote Scripture, and law, and morality and reason and practicality. The devil can use the public conscience of his time. He does in wars, in racial and religious persecutions; he did in the Spain of the Inquisition; he does in the American lynching.

For there is nothing so bad but it can masquerade as moral. Conquerors have gone forth with the blessing of popes; a nation invokes its God before beginning a campaign of murder, rape and pillage. The ruthless exploitation of India becomes the civilizing fulfilment of the "white man's burden"; not infrequently the missionary, drummer, and prospector are embodied in one man. In the nineteenth century church, press and university devoted no inconsiderable part of their time to proving the high moral and scientific justice of child labor and human sweating. It is a matter of record that chattel slavery in this country was deduced from Biblical injunction, that the universities furnished brains for its defense. Surely Bernard Shaw was not describing the Englishman alone when he said in "The Man of Destiny" that ". . . you will never find an Englishman in the wrong. He does everything on principle. He fights you on patriotic principles; he robs you on business principles. . . ."

Liberty, equality, fraternity—what a grotesque career those words have had. Almost every attempt to mitigate the hardships of industrialism has had to deal with the bogey of liberty. Labor organization, factory laws, health regulations are still fought as infringements of liberty. And in the name of equality what fantasies of taxation have we not woven? what travesties of justice set up? "The law in its majestic equality," writes Anatole France, "forbids the rich as well as the poor to sleep in the streets and to steal bread." Fraternity becomes the hypocritical slogan by which we refuse to enact what is called "class legislation"—a policy which in theory denies the existence of classes, in practice legislates in favor of the rich. The laws which go unchallenged are laws friendly to business; class legislation means working-class legislation.

You have to go among lawyers to see this idolatrous process in its most perfect form. When a judge sets out to "interpret" the Constitution, what is it that he does? He takes a sentence written by a group of men more than a hundred years ago. That sentence expressed their policy about certain conditions which they had to deal with. In it was summed up what they intended to do about the problems they saw. That is all the sentence means. But in the course of a century new problems arise—problems the Fathers could no more have foreseen than we can foresee the problems of the year two thousand. Yet that sentence which contained their wisdom about particular events has acquired an emotional force which persists long after the events have passed away. Legends gather about the men who wrote it: those legends are absorbed by us almost with our mothers' milk. We never again read that sentence straight. It has a gravity out of all proportion to its use, and we call it a fundamental principle of government. Whatever we want to do is hallowed and justified, if it can be made to appear as a deduction from that sentence. To put new wine in old bottles is one of the aims of legal casuistry.

Reformers practice it. You hear it said that the initiative

and referendum are a return to the New England town meeting. That is supposed to be an argument for direct legislation. But surely the analogy is superficial; the difference profound. The infinitely greater complexity of legislation today, the vast confusion in the aims of the voting population, produce a difference of so great a degree that it amounts to a difference in kind. The naturalist may classify the dog and the fox, the house-cat and the tiger together for certain purposes. The historian of political forms may see in the town meeting a forerunner of direct legislation. But no housewife dare classify the cat and the tiger, the dog and the fox, as the same kind of animal. And no statesman can argue the virtues of the referendum from the successes of the town meeting.

But the propagandists do it nevertheless, and their propaganda thrives upon it. The reason is simple. The town meeting is an obviously respectable institution, glorified by all the reverence men give to the dead. It has acquired the seal of an admired past, and any proposal that can borrow that seal can borrow that reverence too. A name trails behind it an army of associations. That army will fight in any cause that bears the name. So the reformers of California, the Lorimerites of Chicago, and the Barnes Republicans of Albany all use the name of Lincoln for their political associations. In the struggle that preceded the Republican Convention of 1912 it was rumored that the Taft reactionaries would put forward Lincoln's son as chairman of the convention in order to counteract Roosevelt's claim that he stood in Lincoln's shoes.

Casuistry is nothing but the injection of your own meaning into an old name. At school when the teacher asked us whether we had studied the lesson, the invariable answer was Yes. We had indeed stared at the page for a few minutes, and that could be called studying. Sometimes the head-master would break into the room just in time to see the conclusion of a scuffle. Jimmy's clothes are white with dust. "Johnny, did you throw chalk at Jimmy?" "No, sir," says Johnny, and then under his breath to placate God's penchant for truth, "I threw the chalk-eraser." Once in Portland, Maine, I ordered iced tea at an hotel. The waitress brought me a glass of yellowish liquid with a two-inch collar of foam at the top. No tea I had ever seen outside of a prohibition state looked like that. Though it was tea, it might have been beer. Perhaps if I had smiled or winked in ordering the tea, it would have been beer. The two looked alike in Portland; they were interchangeable. You could drink tea and fool yourself into thinking it was beer. You could drink beer and pass for a tea-toper.

It is rare, I think, that the fraud is so genial and so deliberate. The openness cleanses it. Advertising, for example, would be nothing but gigantic and systematic lying if almost everybody didn't know that it was. Yet it runs into the sinister all the time. The pure food agitation is largely an effort to make the label and the contents tell the same story. It was noteworthy that, following the discovery of salvarsan or "606" by Dr. Ehrlich, the quack doctors began to call their treatments "606." But the deliberate casuistry of lawyers, quacks, or politicians is not so difficult to deal with. The very deliberation makes it easier to detect, for it is generally awkward. What one man can consciously devise, other men can understand.

But unconscious casuistry deceives us all. No one escapes it entirely. A wealth of evidence could be adduced to support this from the studies of dreams and fantasies made by the Freudian school of psychologists. They have shown how constantly the mind cloaks a deep meaning in a shallow incident—how the superficial is all the time being shoved into the light of consciousness in order to conceal a buried intention; how inveterate is our use of symbols.

Between ourselves and our real natures we interpose that wax figure of idealizations and selections which we call our character. We extend this into all our thinking. Between us and the realities of social life we build up a mass of generalizations, abstract ideas, ancient glories, and personal wishes. They simplify and soften experience. It is so much easier to talk of poverty than to think of the poor, to argue the rights of capital than to see its results. Pretty soon we come to think of the theories and abstract ideas as things in themselves. We worry about their fate and forget their original content.

For words, theories, symbols, slogans, abstractions of all kinds are nothing but the porous vessels into which life flows, is contained for a time, and then passes through. But our reverence clings to the vessels. The old meaning may have disappeared, a new one come in—no matter, we try to believe there has been no change. And when life's expansion demands some new container, nothing is more difficult than the realization that the old vessels cannot be stretched to the present need.

It is interesting to notice how in the very act of analyzing it I have fallen into this curious and ancient habit. My point is that the metaphor is taken for the reality: I have used at least six metaphors to state it. Abstractions are not cloaks, nor wax figures, nor walls, nor vessels, and life doesn't flow like water. What they really are you and I know inwardly by using abstractions and living our lives. But once I attempt to give that inwardness expression, I must use the only weapons I have—abstractions, theories, phrases. By an effort of the sympathetic imagination you can revive within yourself something of my inward sense. As I have had to abstract from life in order to communicate, so you are compelled to animate my abstractions, in order to understand.

I know of no other method of communication between two people. Language is always grossly inadequate. It is inadequate if the listener is merely passive, if he falls into the mistake of the literal-minded who expect words to contain a precise image of reality. They never do. All language can achieve is to act as a guidepost to the imagination enabling the reader to recreate the author's insight. The artist does that: he controls his medium so that we come most readily to the heart of his intention. In the lyric poet the control is often so delicate that the hearer lives over again the finely shaded mood of the poet. Take the words of a lyric for what they say, and they say nothing most of the time. And that is true of philosophers. You must penetrate the ponderous vocabulary, the professional cant to the insight beneath or you scoff at the mountain ranges of words and phrases. It is this that Bergson means when he tells us that a philosopher's intuition always outlasts his system. Unless you get at that you remain forever foreign to the thinker.

That too is why debating is such a wretched amusement and most partisanship, most controversy, so degrading. The trick here is to argue from the opponent's language, never from his insight. You take him literally, you pick up his sentences, and you show what nonsense they are. You do not try to weigh what you see against what he sees; you contrast what you see with what he says. So debating becomes a way of confirming your own prejudices; it is never, never in any debate I have suffered through, a search for understanding from the angles of two differing insights.

And, of course, in those more sinister forms of debating, court trials, where the stakes are so much bigger, the skill of a successful lawyer is to make the atmosphere as opaque as possible to the other lawyer's contention. Men have been hanged as a result. How often in a political campaign does a candidate suggest that behind the platforms and speeches of his opponents there might be some new and valuable understanding of the country's need?

The fact is that we argue and quarrel an enormous lot over words. Our prevailing habit is to think about phrases, "ideals," theories, not about the realities they express. In controversy we do not try to find our opponent's meaning: we examine his vocabulary. And in our own efforts to shape policies we do not seek out what is worth doing: we seek out what will pass for moral, practical, popular or constitutional.

In this the Vice Commission reflected our national habits. For those earnest men and women in Chicago did not set out to find a way of abolishing prostitution; they set out to find a way that would conform to four idols they worshiped. The only cure for prostitution might prove to be "immoral," "impractical," unconstitutional, and unpopular. I suspect that it is. But the honest thing to do would have been to look for that cure without preconceived notions. Having found it, the Commission could then have said to the public: "This is what will cure the social evil. It means these changes in industry, sex relations, law and public opinion. If you think it is worth the cost you can begin to deal with the problem. If you don't, then confess that you will not abolish prostitution, and turn your compassion to softening its effects."

That would have left the issues clear and wholesome. But the procedure of the Commission is a blow to honest thinking. Its conclusions may "square with the public conscience of the American people" but they will not square with the intellectual conscience of anybody. To tell you at the top of the page that absolute annihilation of prostitution is the ultimate ideal and twenty lines further on that the method must be constitutional is nothing less than an insult to the intelligence. Calf-worship was never more idolatrous than this. Truth would have slept more comfortably in Procrustes' bed.

Let no one imagine that I take the four preconceived ideas of the Commission too seriously. On the first reading of the report they aroused no more interest in me than the ordinary lip-honor we all do to conventionality—I had heard of the great fearlessness of this report, and I supposed that this bending of the knee was nothing but the innocent hypocrisy of the reformer who wants to make his proposal not too shocking. But it was a mistake. Those four idols really dominated the minds of the Commission, and without them the report cannot be understood. They are typical idols of the American people. This report offers an opportunity to see the concrete results of worshiping them.

A valuable contribution, then, must be *moral*. There is no doubt that the Commission means sexually moral. We Americans always use the word in that limited sense. If you say that Jones is a moral man you mean that he is faithful to his wife. He may support her by selling pink pills; he is nevertheless moral if he is monogamous. The average American rarely speaks of industrial piracy as immoral. He may condemn it, but not with that word. If he extends the meaning of immoral at all, it is to the vices most closely allied to sex—drink and gambling.

Now sexual morality is pretty clearly defined for the Commission. As we have seen, it means that sex must be confined to procreation by a healthy, intelligent and strictly monogamous couple. All other sexual expression would come under the ban of disapproval. I am sure I do the Commission no injustice. Now this limited conception of sex has had a disastrous effect: it has forced the Commission to ignore the sexual impulse in discussing a sexual problem. Any modification of the relationship of men and women was immediately put out of consideration. Such suggestions as Forel, Ellen Key, or Havelock Ellis make could, of course, not even get a hearing.

With this moral ideal in mind, not only vice, but sex itself, becomes an evil thing. Hence the hysterical and minute application of the taboo wherever sex shows itself. Barred from any reform which would reabsorb the impulse into civilized life, the Commissioners had no other course but to hunt it, as an outlaw. And in doing this they were compelled to discard the precious values of art, religion and social life of which this superfluous energy is the creator. Driven to think of it as bad, except for certain particular functions, they could, of course, not see its possibilities. Hence the poverty of their suggestions along educational and artistic lines.

A valuable contribution, we are told, must be *reasonable* and *practical*. Here is a case where words cannot be taken literally. "Reasonable" in America certainly never even pretended to mean in accordance with a rational ideal, and "practical,"—well one thinks of "practical politics," "practical business men," and "unpractical reformers." Boiled down these words amount to something like this: the proposals must not be new or startling; must not involve any radical disturbance of any respectable person's selfishness; must not call forth any great opposition; must look definite and immediate; must be tangible like a raid, or a jail, or the paper of an ordinance, or a policeman's club. Above all a "reasonable and practical" proposal must not require any imaginative patience. The actual proposals have all these qualities: if they are "reasonable and practical" then we know by a good demonstration what these terms meant to that average body of citizens.

To see that is to see exposed an important facet of the American temperament. Our dislike of "talk"; the frantic desire to "do something" without inquiring whether it is worth doing; the dollar standard; the unwillingness to cast any bread upon the waters; our preference for a sparrow in the hand to a forest of song-birds; the naïve inability to understand the inner satisfactions of bankrupt poets and the unworldliness of eccentric thinkers; success—mania; philistinism—they are pieces of the same cloth. They come from failure or unwillingness to project the mind beyond the daily routine of things, to play over the whole horizon of possibilities, and to recognize that all is not said when we have spoken. In those words "reasonable and practical" is the Chinese Wall of America, that narrow boundary which contracts our vision to the moment, cuts us off from the culture of the world, and makes us such provincial, unimaginative blunderers over our own problems. Fixation upon the immediate has made a rich country poor in leisure, has in a land meant for liberal living incited an insane struggle for existence. One suspects at times that our national cult of optimism is no real feeling that the world is good, but a fear that pessimism will produce panics.

How this fascination of the obvious has balked the work of the Commission I need not elaborate. That the long process of civilizing sex received perfunctory attention; that the imaginative value of sex was lost in a dogma; that the implied changes in social life were dodged—all that has been pointed out. It was the inability to rise above the immediate that makes the report read as if the policeman were the only agent of civilization.

For where in the report is any thorough discussion by sociologists of the relations of business and marriage to vice? Why is there no testimony by psychologists to show how sex can be affected by environment, by educators to show how it can be trained, by industrial experts to show how monotony and fatigue affect it? Where are the detailed proposals by specialists, for decent housing and working conditions, for educational reform, for play facilities? The Commission wasn't afraid of details: didn't it recommend searchlights in the parks as a weapon against vice? Why then isn't there a budget, a large, comprehensive budget, precise and informing, in which provision is made for beginning to civilize Chicago? That wouldn't have been "reasonable and practical," I presume, for it would have cost millions and millions of dollars. And where would the money have come from? Were the single-taxers, the Socialists consulted? But their proposals would require big changes in property interests, and would that be "reasonable and practical"? Evidently not: it is more reasonable and practical to keep park benches out of the shadows and to plague unescorted prostitutes.

And where are the open questions: the issues that everybody should consider, the problems that scientists should study? I see almost no trace of them. Why are the sexual problems not even stated? Where are the doubts that should have honored these investigations, the frank statement of all the gaps in knowledge, and the obscurities in morals? Knowing perfectly well that vice will not be repressed within a year or prostitution absolutely annihilated in ten, it might, I should think, have seemed more important that the issues be made clear and the thought of the people fertilized than that the report should look very definite and precise. There are all sorts of things we do not understand about this problem. The opportunities for study which the Commissioners had must have made these empty spaces evident. Why then were we not taken into their confidence? Along what lines is investigation most needed? To what problems, what issues, shall we give our attention? What is the debatable ground in this territory? The Commission does not say, and I for one, ascribe the silence to the American preoccupation with immediate, definite, tangible interests.

Wells has written penetratingly about this in "The New Machiavelli." I have called this fixation on the nearest object at hand an American habit. Perhaps as Mr. Wells shows it is an English one too. But in this country we have a philosophy to express it—the philosophy of the Reasonable and the Practical, and so I do not hesitate to import Mr. Wells's observations: "It has been the chronic mistake of statecraft and all organizing spirits to attempt immediately to scheme and arrange and achieve. Priests, schools of thought, political schemers, leaders of men, have always slipped into the error of assuming that they can think out the whole—or at any rate completely think out definite parts—of the purpose and future of man, clearly and finally; they have set themselves to legislate and construct on that assumption, and, experiencing the perplexing obduracy and evasions of reality, they have taken to dogma, persecution, training, pruning, secretive education; and all the stupidities of self-sufficient energy. In the passion of their good intentions they have not hesitated to conceal facts, suppress thought, crush disturbing initiatives and apparently detrimental desires. And so it is blunderingly and wastefully, destroying with the making, that any extension of social organization is at present achieved. Directly, however, this idea of an emancipation from immediacy is grasped, directly the dominating importance of this critical, less personal, mental hinterland in the individual and of the collective mind in the race is understood, the whole problem of the statesman and his attitude toward politics gains a new significance, and becomes accessible to a new series of solutions. . . ."

Let no one suppose that the unwillingness to cultivate what Mr. Wells calls the "mental hinterland" is a vice peculiar to the business man. The colleges submit to it whenever they concentrate their attention on the details of the student's vocation before they have built up some cultural background. The whole drift towards industrial training in schools has the germs of disaster within it—a preoccupation with the technique of a career. I am not a lover of the "cultural" activities of our schools and colleges, still less am I a lover of shallow specialists. The unquestioned need for experts in politics is full of the very real danger that detailed preparation may give us a bureaucracy—a government by men divorced from human tradition. The churches submit to the demand for immediacy with great alacrity. Look at the so-called "liberal" churches. Reacting against an empty formalism they are tumbling over themselves to prove how directly they touch daily life. You read glowing articles in magazines about preachers who devote their time to housing reforms, milk supplies, the purging of the civil service. If you lament the ugliness of their churches, the poverty of the ritual, and the political absorption of their sermons, you are told that the church must abandon forms and serve the common life of men. There are many ways of serving everyday needs,—turning churches into social reform organs and political rostra is, it seems to me, an obvious but shallow way of performing that service. When churches cease to paint the background of our lives, to nourish a Weltanschauung, strengthen men's ultimate purposes and reaffirm the deepest values of life, then churches have ceased to meet the needs for which they exist. That "hinterland" affects daily life, and the church which cannot get a leverage on it by any other method than entering into immediate political controversy is simply a church that is dead. It may be an admirable agent of reform, but it has ceased to be a church.

A large wing of the Socialist Party is the slave of obvious success. It boasts that it has ceased to be "visionary" and has become "practical." Votes, winning campaigns, putting through reform measures seem a great achievement. It forgets the difference between voting the Socialist ticket and understanding Socialism. The vote is the tangible thing, and for that these Socialist politicians work. They get the votes, enough to elect them to office. In the City of Schenectady that happened as a result of the mayoralty campaign of 1911. I had an opportunity to observe the results. A few Socialists were in office set to govern a city with no Socialist "hinterland." It was a pathetic situation, for any reform proposal had to pass the judgment of men and women who did not see life as the officials did. On no important measure could the administration expect popular understanding. What was the result? In crucial issues, like taxation, the Socialists had to submit to the ideas,—the general state of mind of the community. They had to reverse their own theories and accept those that prevailed in that unconverted city. I wondered over our helplessness, for I was during a period one of those officials. The other members of the administration used to say at every opportunity that we were fighting "The Beast" or "Special Privilege." But to me it always seemed that we were like Peer Gynt struggling against the formless Boyg—invisible yet everywhere—we were struggling with the unwatered hinterland of the citizens of Schenectady. I understood then, I think, what Wells meant when he said that he wanted "no longer to 'fix up,' as people say, human affairs, but to devote his forces to the development of that needed intellectual life without which all his shallow attempts at fixing up are futile." For in the last analysis the practical and the reasonable are little idols of day that thwart our efforts.

The third requirement of a valuable contribution, says the Chicago Commission, is the constitutional sanction. This idol carries its own criticism with it. The worship of the constitution amounts, of course, to saying that men exist for the sake of the constitution. The person who holds fast to that idea is forever incapable of understanding either men or constitutions. It is a prime way of making laws ridiculous; if you want to cultivate *lèse-majesté* in Germany get the Kaiser to proclaim his divine origin; if you want to promote disrespect of the courts, announce their infallibility.

But in this case, the Commission is not representative of the dominant thought of our times. The vital part of the population has pretty well emerged from any dumb acquiescence in constitutions. Theodore Roosevelt, who reflects so much of America, has very definitely cast down this idol. Now since he stands generally some twenty years behind the pioneer and about six months ahead of the majority, we may rest assured that this much-needed iconoclasm is in process of achievement.

Closely related to the constitution and just as decadent to-day are the Sanctity of Private Property, Vested Rights, Competition the Life of Trade, Prosperity (at any cost). Each one of these ideas was born of an original need, served its historical function and survived beyond its allotted time. Nowadays you still come across some of these ancient notions, especially in courts, where they do no little damage in perverting justice, but they are ghost-like and disreputable, gibbering and largely helpless. He who is watching the ascendant ideas of American life can afford to feel that the early maxims of capitalism are doomed.

But the habit of mind which would turn an instrument of life into an immutable law of its existence—that habit is always with us. We may outgrow our adoration of the Constitution or Private Property only to establish some new totem pole. In the arts we call this inveterate tendency classicalism. It is, of course, a habit by no means confined to the arts. Politics, religion, science are subject to it,—in politics we call it conservative, in religion orthodox, in science we describe it as academic. Its manifestations are multiform but they have a common source. An original creative impulse of the mind expresses itself in a certain formula; posterity mistakes the formula for the impulse. A genius will use his medium in a particular way because it serves his need; this way becomes a fixed rule which the classicalist serves. It has been pointed out that because the first steam trains were run on roads built for carts and coaches, the railway gauge almost everywhere in the world became fixed at four feet eight and one-half inches.

Some Necessary Iconoclasm

You might say that genius works inductively and finds a method; the conservative works deductively from the method and defeats whatever genius he may have. A friend of mine had written a very brilliant article on a play which had puzzled New York. Some time later I was discussing the article with another friend of a decidedly classicalist bent. "What is it?" he protested, "it isn't criticism for it's half rhapsody; it isn't rhapsody because it is analytical. . . . What is it? That's what I want to know." "But isn't it fine, and worth having, and aren't you glad it was written?" I pleaded. "Well, if I knew what it was. . . ." And so the argument ran for hours. Until he had subsumed the article under certain categories he had come to accept, appreciation was impossible for him. I have many arguments with my classicalist friend. This time it was about George Moore's "Ave." I was trying to express my delight. "It isn't a novel, or an essay, or a real confession—it's nothing," said he. His well-ordered mind was compelled to throw out of doors any work for which he had no carefully prepared pocket. I thought of Aristotle, who denied the existence of a mule because it was neither a horse nor an ass.

Dramatic critics follow Aristotle in more ways than one. A play is produced which fascinates an audience for weeks. It is published and read all over the world. Then you are treated to endless discussions by the critics trying to prove that "it is not a play." So-and-so-and-so constitute a play, they affirm,—this thing doesn't meet the requirements, so away with it. They forget that nobody would have had the slightest idea what a play was if plays hadn't been written; that the rules deduced from the plays that have already been written are no eternal law for the plays that will be.

Classicalism and invention are irreconcilable enemies. Let it be understood that I am not decrying the great nourishment which a living tradition offers. The criticism I am making is of those who try to feed upon the husks alone. Without the slightest paradox one may say that the classicalist is most foreign to the classics. He does not put himself within the creative impulses of the past: he is blinded by their manifestations. It is perhaps no accident that two of the greatest classical scholars in England—Gilbert Murray and Alfred Zimmern—are political radicals. The man whom I call here the classicalist cannot possibly be creative, for the essence of his creed is that there must be nothing new under the sun.

The United States, you imagine, would of all nations be the freest from classicalism. Settled as a great adventure and dedicated to an experiment in republicanism, the tradition of the country is of extending boundaries, obstacles overcome, and pioneering exploits in which a wilderness was subdued to human uses. The very air of America would seem to be a guarantee against formalism. You would think that self-government finds its surest footing here—that real autonomy of the spirit which makes human uses the goal of effort, denies all inhuman ideals, seeks out what men want, and proceeds to create it. With such a history how could a nation fail to see in its constitution anything but a tool of life, like the axe, the spade or the plough?

The West has in a measure carried its freedom over into politics and social life generally. Formalism sets in as you move east and south into the older and more settled communities. There the pioneering impulse has passed out of

life into stupid history books, and the inevitable classicalism, the fear of adventure, the superstition before social
invention, have reasserted themselves. If I may turn for a
moment from description to prophecy, it is to say that this
equilibrium will not hold for very long. There are signs that
the West after achieving the reforms which it needs to-
day—reforms which will free its economic life from the
credit monopolies of the East, and give it a greater fluidity
in the marketing of its products—will follow the way of all
agricultural communities to a rural and placid conservatism.
The spirit of the pioneer does not survive forever: it is kept
alive to-day, I believe, by certain unnatural irritants which
may be summed up as absentee ownership. The West is suffering from foreignly owned railroads, power-resources,
and an alien credit control. But once it recaptures these essentials of its economic life, once the "progressive" movement is victorious, I venture to predict that the agricultural
West will become the heart of American complacency. The
East, on the other hand, with its industrial problem must go
to far more revolutionary measures for a solution. And the
East is fertilized continually by European traditions: that
stream of immigration brings with it a thousand unforesee-
able possibilities. The great social adventure of America is
no longer the conquest of the wilderness but the absorption
of fifty different peoples. To-day perhaps, it is still predominantly a question for the East. But it means that America is
turning from the contrast between her courage and nature's
obstacles to a comparison of her civilization with Europe's.
Immigration more than anything else is drawing us into
world problems. Many people profess to see horrible dan-

gers in the foreign invasion. Certainly no man is sure of its conclusion. It may swamp us, it may, if we seize the opportunity, mean the impregnation of our national life with a new brilliancy.

I have said that the West is still moved by the tapering impulse of the pioneer, and I have ventured to predict that this would soon dwindle into an agricultural toryism. That prediction may very easily be upset. Far-reaching mechanical inventions already threaten to transform farming into an industry. I refer to those applications of power to agriculture which will inevitably divorce the farmer from the ownership of his tools. An industrial revolution analogous to that in manufacture during the nineteenth century is distinctly probable, and capitalistic agriculture may soon cease to be a contradiction in terms. Like all inventions it will disturb deeply the classicalist tendency, and this disturbance may generate a new impulse to replace the decadent one of the pioneer.

Without some new dynamic force America, for all her tradition, is not immune to a hardening formalism. The psychological descent into classicalism is always a strong possibility. That is why we, the children of frontiersmen, city builders and immigrants, surprise Europe constantly with our worship of constitutions, our social and political timidity. In many ways we are more defenceless against these deadening habits than the people of Europe. Our geographical isolation preserves us from any vivid sense of national contrast: our imaginations are not stirred by different civilizations. We have almost no spiritual weapons against classicalism: universities, churches, newspapers are by-products of a commercial success; we have no tradition of intellectual revolt. The American college student has the gravity and mental habits of a Supreme Court judge; his "wild oats" are rarely spiritual; the critical, analytical habit of mind is distrusted. We say that "knocking" is a sign of the "sorehead" and we sublimate criticism by saying that "every knock is a boost." America does not play with ideas; generous speculation is regarded as insincere, and shunned as if it might endanger the optimism which underlies success. All this becomes such an insulation against new ideas that when the Yankee goes abroad he takes his environment with him.

It seems at times as if our capacity for appreciating originality were absorbed in the trivial eccentricities of fads and fashions. The obvious novelties of machinery and locomotion, phonographs and yellow journalism slake the American thirst for creation pretty thoroughly. In serious matters we follow the Vice Commission's fourth essential of a valuable contribution—*that which will square with the public conscience of the American people.*

I do not care to dilate upon the exploded pretensions of Mr. and Mrs. Grundy. They are a fairly disreputable couple by this time because we are beginning to know how much morbidity they represent. The Vice Commission, for example, bowed to what might be called the "instinctive conscience" of America when it balked at tracing vice to its source in the over-respected institutions of American life and the over-respected natures of American men and women. It bowed to the prevailing conscience when it proposed taboos instead of radical changes. It bowed to a traditional conscience when it confused the sins of sex with the possibilities of sex; and it paid tribute to a verbal conscience, to a lip morality, when, with extreme irrelevance to its beloved police, it proclaimed "absolute annihilation" the ultimate ideal. In brief, the commission failed to see that the working conscience of America is to-day bound up with the very evil it is supposed to eradicate by a relentless warfare.

It was to be expected. Our conscience is not the vessel of eternal verities. It grows with our social life, and a new social condition means a radical change in conscience. In order to do away with vice America must live and think and feel differently. This is an old story. Because of it all innovators have been at war with the public conscience of their time. Yet there is nothing strange or particularly disheartening about this commonplace observation: to expect anything else is to hope that a nation will lift itself by its own bootstraps. Yet there is danger the moment leaders of the people make a virtue of homage to the unregenerate, public conscience.

In La Follette's Magazine (Feb. 17, 1912) there is a leading article called "The Great Issue." You can read there that "the composite judgment is always safer and wiser and stronger and more unselfish than the judgment of any one individual mind. The people have been betrayed by their representatives again and again. The real danger to democracy lies not in the ignorance or want of patriotism of the people, but in the corrupting influence of powerful business organizations upon the representatives of the people. . . ."

I have only one quarrel with that philosophy—its negativity. With the belief that government is futile and mischievous unless supported by the mass of the people; with the undeniable fact that business has corrupted public officials—I have no complaint. What I object to is the emphasis which shifts the blame for our troubles from the shoulders of the people to those of the "corrupting interests." For this seems to me nothing but the resuscitation of the devil: when things go wrong it is somebody else's fault. We are peculiarly open to this kind of vanity in America. If some wise law is passed we say it is the will of the people showing its power of self-government. But if that will is so weak and timid that a great evil like child labor persists to our shame we turn the responsibility over to the devil personified as a "special interest." It is an old habit of the race which seems to have begun with the serpent in the Garden of Eden.

The word demagogue has been frightfully maltreated in late years, but surely here is its real meaning—to flatter the people by telling them that their failures are somebody else's fault. For if a nation declares it has reached its majority by instituting self-government, then it cannot shirk responsibility.

These "special interests"—big business, a corrupt press, crooked politics—grew up within the country, were promoted by American citizens, admired by millions of them, and acquiesced in by almost all of them. Whoever thinks that business corruption is the work of a few inhumanly cunning individuals with monstrous morals is self-righteous without excuse. Capitalists did not violate the public conscience of America; they expressed it. That conscience was inadequate and unintelligent. We are being pinched by the acts it nourished. A great outcry has arisen and a number of perfectly conventional men like Lorimer suffer an undeserved humiliation. We say it is a "moral awakening." That is another dodge by which we pretend that we were always wise and just, though a trifle sleepy. In reality we are witnessing a change of conscience, initiated by cranks and fanatics, sustained for a long time by minorities, which has at last infected the mass of the people.

The danger I spoke of arises just here: the desire to infect at once the whole mass crowds out the courage of the innovator. No man can do his best work if he bows at every step to the public conscience of his age. The real service to democracy is the fullest, freest expression of talent. The best servants of the people, like the best valets, must whisper unpleasant truths in the master's ear. It is the court fool, not the foolish courtier, whom the king can least afford to lose.

Hostile critics of democracy have long pointed out that mediocrity becomes the rule. They have not been without facts for their support. And I do not see why we who believe in democracy should not recognize this danger and trace it to its source. Certainly it is not answered with a sneer. I have worked in the editorial office of a popular magazine, a magazine that is known widely as a champion of popular rights. By personal experience, by intimate conversations, and by looking about, I think I am pretty well aware of what the influence of business upon journalism amounts to. I have seen the inside working of business pressure; articles of my own have been suppressed after they were in type; friends of mine have told me stories of expurgation, of the "morganization" of their editorial policy. And in the face of that I should like to record it as my sincere conviction that no financial power is one-tenth so corrupting, so insidious, so hostile to originality and frank statement as the fear of the public which reads the magazine. For one item suppressed out of respect for a railroad or a bank, nine are rejected because of the prejudices of the public. This will anger the farmers, that will arouse the Catholics, another will shock the summer girl. Anybody can take a fling at poor old Mr. Rockefeller, but the great mass of average citizens (to which none of us belongs) must be left in undisturbed possession of its prejudices. In that subservience, and not in the meddling of Mr. Morgan, is the reason why American journalism is so flaccid, so repetitious and so dull.

The people should be supreme, yes, its will should be the law of the land. But it is a caricature of democracy to make it also the law of individual initiative. One thing it is to say that all proposals must ultimately win the acceptance of the majority; it is quite another to propose nothing which is not immediately acceptable. It is as true of the nation as of the body that one leg cannot go forward very far unless the whole body follows. That is a different thing from trying to move both legs forward at the same time. The one is democracy; the other is—demolatry.

It is better to catch the idol-maker than to smash each idol. It would be an endless task to hunt down all the masks, the will-o'-the-wisps and the shadows which divert us from our real purpose. Each man carries within himself the cause of his own mirages. Whenever we accept an idea as authority instead of as instrument, an idol is set up. We worship the plough, and not the fruit. And from this habit there is no permanent escape. Only effort can keep the mind centered truly. Whenever criticism slackens, whenever we sink into acquiescence, the mind swerves aside and clings with the gratitude of the weary to some fixed idea. It is so much easier to follow a rule of thumb, and obey the constitution, than to find out what we really want and to do it.

A great deal of political theory has been devoted to asking: what is the aim of government? Many readers may have wondered why that question has not figured in these pages. For the logical method would be to decide upon the ultimate ideal of statecraft and then elaborate the technique of its realization. I have not done that because this rational procedure inverts the natural order of things and develops all kinds of theoretical tangles and pseudo-problems. They come from an effort to state abstractly in intellectual terms qualities that can be known only by direct experience. You achieve nothing but confusion if you begin by announcing that politics must achieve "justice" or "liberty" or "happiness." Even though you are perfectly sure that you know exactly what these words mean translated into concrete experiences, it is very doubtful whether you can really convey your meaning to anyone else. "Plaisante justice qu'une rivière borne. Vérité, au deçà des Pyrénées, erreur au de là," says Pascal. If what is good in the world depended on our ability to define it we should be hopeless indeed.

This is an old difficulty in ethics. Many men have remarked that we quarrel over the "problem of evil," never over the "problem of good." That comes from the fact that good is a quality of experience which does not demand an explanation. When we are thwarted we begin to ask why. It was the evil in the world that set Leibniz the task of justifying the ways of God to man. Nor is it an accident that in daily life misfortune turns men to philosophy. One might generalize and say that as soon as we begin to explain, it is because we have been made to complain.

No moral judgment can decide the value of life. No ethical theory can announce any intrinsic good. The whole speculation about morality is an effort to find a way of living which men who live it will instinctively feel is good. No formula can express an ultimate experience; no axiom can ever be a substitute for what really makes life worth living. Plato may describe the objects which man rejoices over, he may guide them to good experiences, but each man in his inward life is a last judgment on all his values.

This amounts to saying that the goal of action is in its final analysis aesthetic and not moral—a quality of feeling instead of conformity to rule. Words like justice, harmony, power, democracy are simply empirical suggestions which may produce the good life. If the practice of them does not produce it then we are under no obligation to follow them, we should be idolatrous fools to do so. Every abstraction, every rule of conduct, every constitution, every law and social arrangement, is an instrument that has no value in itself. Whatever credit it receives, whatever reverence we give it, is derived from its utility in ministering to those concrete experiences which are as obvious and as undefinable as color or sound. We can celebrate the positively good things, we can live them, we can create them, but we cannot philosophize about them. To the anaesthetic intellect we could not convey the meaning of joy. A creature that could reason but not feel would never know the value of life, for what is ultimate is in itself inexplicable.

Politics is not concerned with prescribing the ultimate qualities of life. When it tries to do so by sumptuary legislation, nothing but mischief is invoked. Its business is to provide opportunities, not to announce ultimate values; to remove oppressive evil and to invent new resources for enjoyment. With the enjoyment itself it can have no concern. That must be lived by each individual. In a sense the politician can never know his own success, for it is registered in men's inner lives, and is largely incommunicable. An increasing harvest of rich personalities is the social reward for a fine statesmanship, but such personalities are free growths in a cordial environment. They cannot be cast in moulds or shaped by law. There is no need, therefore, to generate dialectical disputes about the final goal of politics. No definition can be just—too precise a one can only deceive us into thinking that our definition is true. Call ultimate values by any convenient name, it is of slight importance which you choose. If only men can keep their minds freed from formalism, idol worship, fixed ideas, and exalted abstractions, politicians need not worry about the language in which the end of our striving is expressed. For with the removal of distracting idols, man's experience becomes the center of thought. And if we think in terms of men, find out what really bothers them, seek to supply what they really want, hold only their experience sacred, we shall find our sanction obvious and unchallenged.

CHAPTER VII

THE MAKING OF CREEDS

Y first course in philosophy was nothing less than a summary of the important systems of thought put forward in Western Europe during the last twenty-six hundred years. Perhaps that is a slight exaggeration—we did gloss over a few centuries in the Middle Ages. For the rest we touched upon all the historic names from Thales to Nietzsche. After about nine weeks of this bewildering transit a friend approached me with a sour look on his face. "You know," he said, "I can't make head or tail out of this business. I agree with each philosopher as we study him. But when we get to the next one, I agree with him too. Yet he generally says the other one was wrong. They can't all be right. Can they now?" I was too much puzzled with the same difficulty to help him.

Somewhat later I began to read the history of political theories. It was a less disinterested study than those sophomore speculations, for I had jumped into a profession which carried me through some of the underground passages of "practical politics" and reformist groups. The tangle of motives and facts and ideas was incredible. I began to feel the force of Mr. John Hobson's remark that "if practical workers for social and industrial reforms continue to ignore principles . . . they will have to pay the price which short-sighted empiricism always pays; with slow, hesitant, and staggering steps, with innumerable false starts and back-slidings, they will move in the dark along an unseen track toward an unseen goal." The political theorists laid some claim to lighting up both the track and the goal, and so I turned to them for help.

Now whoever has followed political theory will have derived perhaps two convictions as a reward. Almost all the thinkers seem to regard their systems as true and binding, and none of these systems are. No matter which one you examine, it is inadequate. You cannot be a Platonist or a Benthamite in politics to-day. You cannot go to any of the great philosophers even for the outlines of a statecraft which shall be fairly complete, and relevant to American life. I returned to the sophomore mood: "Each of these thinkers has contributed something, has had some wisdom about events. Looked at in bulk the philosophers can't all be right or all wrong."

But like so many theoretical riddles, this one rested on a very simple piece of ignorance. The trouble was that without realizing it I too had been in search of the philosopher's stone. I too was looking for something that could not be found. That happened in this case to be nothing less than an absolutely true philosophy of politics. It was the old indolence of hoping that somebody had done the world's thinking once and for all. I had conjured up the fantasy of a system which would contain the whole of life, be as reliable as a table of logarithms, foresee all possible emergencies and offer entirely trustworthy rules of action. When it seemed that no such system had ever been produced, I was on the point of damning the entire tribe of theorists from Plato to Marx.

This is what one may call the naïveté of the intellect. Its hope is that some man living at one place on the globe in a particular epoch will, through the miracle of genius, be able to generalize his experience for all time and all space. It says in effect that there is never anything essentially new under the sun, that any moment of experience sufficiently understood would be seen to contain all history and all destiny—that the intellect reasoning on one piece of experience could know what all the rest of experience was like. Looked at more closely this philosophy means that novelty is an illusion of ignorance, that life is an endless repetition, that when you know one revolution of it, you know all the rest. In a very real sense the world has no history and no future, the race has no career. At any moment everything is given: our reason could know that moment so thoroughly that all the rest of life would be like the commuter's who travels back and forth on the same line every day. There would be no inventions and no discoveries, for in the instant that reason had found the key of experience everything would be unfolded. The present would not be the womb of the future: nothing would be embryonic, nothing would *grow*. Experience would cease to be an adventure in order to become the monotonous fulfilment of a perfect prophecy.

This omniscience of the human intellect is one of the commonest assumptions in the world. Although when you state the belief as I have, it sounds absurdly pretentious, yet the boastfulness is closer to the child's who stretches out its hand for the moon than the romantic egotist's who thinks he has created the moon and all the stars. Whole systems of philosophy have claimed such an eternal and absolute validity; the nineteenth century produced a bumper crop of so-called atheists, materialists and determinists who believed in all sincerity that "Science" was capable of a complete truth and unfailing prediction. If you want to see this faith in all its naïveté go into those quaint rationalist circles where Herbert Spencer's ghost announces the "laws of life," with only a few inessential details omitted.

Now, of course, no philosophy of this sort has ever realized such hopes. Mankind has certainly come nearer to justifying Mr. Chesterton's observation that one of its favorite games is called "Cheat the Prophet." . . . "The players listen very carefully and respectfully to all that the clever men have to say about what is to happen in the next generation. The players then wait until all the clever men are dead, and bury them nicely. They then go and do something else." Now this weakness is not, as Mr. Chesterton would like to believe, confined to the clever men. But it is a weakness, and many people have speculated about it. Why in the face of hundreds of philosophies wrecked on the rocks of the unexpected do men continue to believe that the intellect can transcend the vicissitudes of experience?

For they certainly do believe it, and generally the more parochial their outlook, the more cosmic their pretensions. All of us at times yearn for the comfort of an absolute philosophy. We try to believe that, however finite we may be, our intellect is something apart from the cycle of our life, capable by an Olympian detachment from human interests of a divine thoroughness. Even our evolutionist philosophy, as Bergson shows, "begins by showing us in the intellect a local effect of evolution, a flame, perhaps accidental, which lights up the coming and going of living things in the narrow passage open to their action; and lo! forgetting what it has just told us, makes of this lantern glimmering in a tunnel a Sun which can illuminate the world."

This is what most of us do in our search for a philosophy of politics. We forget that the big systems of theory are much more like village lamp-posts than they are like the sun, that they were made to light up a particular path, obviate certain dangers, and aid a peculiar mode of life. The understanding of the place of theory in life is a comparatively new one. We are just beginning to see how creeds are made. And the insight is enormously fertile. Thus Mr. Alfred Zimmern in his fine study of "The Greek Commonwealth" says of Plato and Aristotle that no interpretation can be satisfactory which does not take into account the impression left upon their minds by the social development which made the age of these philosophers a period of Athenian decline. Mr. Zimmern's approach is common enough in modern scholarship, but the full significance of it for the creeds we ourselves are making is still something of a novelty. When we are asked to think of the "Republic" as the reaction of decadent Greece upon the conservative temperament of Plato, the function of theory is given a new illumination. Political philosophy at once appears as a human invention in a particular crisis—an instrument to fit a need. The pretension to finality falls away.

This is a great emancipation. Instead of clinging to the naïve belief that Plato was legislating for all mankind, you can discuss his plans as a temporary superstructure made for an historical purpose. You are free then to appreciate the more enduring portions of his work, to understand Santayana when he says of the Platonists, "their theories are so extravagant, yet their wisdom seems so great. Platonism is a very refined and beautiful expression of our natural instincts, it embodies conscience and utters our inmost hopes." This insight into the values of human life, partial though it be, is what constitutes the abiding monument of Plato's genius. His constructions, his formal creeds, his law-making and social arrangements are local and temporary— for us they can have only an antiquarian interest.

In some such way as this the sophomoric riddle is answered: no thinker can lay down a course of action for all mankind—programs if they are useful at all are useful for some particular historical period. But if the thinker sees at all deeply into the life of his own time, his theoretical system will rest upon observation of human nature. That remains as a residue of wisdom long after his reasoning and his concrete program have passed into limbo. For human nature in all its profounder aspects changes very little in the few generations since our Western wisdom has come to be recorded. These *aperçus* left over from the great speculations are the golden threads which successive thinkers weave into the pattern of their thought. Wisdom remains; theory passes.

If that is true of Plato with his ample vision how much truer is it of the theories of the littler men—politicians, courtiers and propagandists who make up the academy of politics. Machiavelli will, of course, be remembered at once as a man, whose speculations were fitted to an historical crisis. His advice to the Prince was real advice, not a sermon. A boss was telling a governor how to extend his power. The wealth of Machiavelli's learning and the splendid penetration of his mind are used to interpret experience for a particular purpose. I have always thought that Machiavelli derives his bad name from a too transparent honesty. Less direct minds would have found high-sounding ethical sanctions in which to conceal the real intent. That was the nauseating method of nineteenth century economists when they tried to identify the brutal practices of capitalism with the beneficence of nature and the Will of God. Not so Machiavelli. He could write without a blush that "a prince, especially a new one, cannot observe all those things for which men are esteemed, being often forced, in order to maintain the state, to act contrary to fidelity, friendship, humanity, and religion." The apologists of business also justified a rupture with human decencies. They too fitted their theory to particular purposes, but they had not the courage to avow it even to themselves.

The rare value of Machiavelli is just this lack of self-deception. You may think his morals devilish, but you cannot accuse him of quoting scripture. I certainly do not admire the end he serves: the extension of an autocrat's power is a frivolous perversion of government. His ideal happens, however, to be the aim of most foreign offices, politicians and "princes of finance." Machiavelli's morals are not one bit worse than the practices of the men who rule the world to-day. An American Senate tore up the Hay-Pauncefote treaty, and with the approval of the President acted "contrary to fidelity" and friendship too; Austria violated the Treaty of Berlin by annexing Bosnia and Herzegovina. Machiavelli's ethics are commonplace enough. His head is clearer than the average. He let the cat out of the bag and showed in the boldest terms how theory becomes an instrument of practice. You may take him as a symbol of the political theorist. You may say that all the thinkers of influence have been writing advice to the Prince. Machiavelli recognized Lorenzo the Magnificent; Marx, the proletariat of Europe.

At first this sounds like standing the world on its head, denying reason and morality, and exalting practice over righteousness. That is neither here nor there. I am simply trying to point out an illuminating fact whose essential truth can hardly be disputed. The important social philosophies are consciously or otherwise the servants of men's purposes. Good or bad, that it seems to me is the way we work. We find reasons for what we want to do. The big men from Machiavelli through Rousseau to Karl Marx brought history, logic, science and philosophy to prop up and strengthen their deepest desires. The followers, the epigones, may accept the reasons of Rousseau and Marx and deduce rules of action from them. But the original genius sees the dynamic purpose first, finds reasons afterward. This amounts to saying that man when he is most creative is not a rational, but a wilful animal.

The political thinker who to-day exercises the greatest influence on the Western World is, I suppose, Karl Marx.

The socialist movement calls him its prophet, and, while many socialists say he is superseded, no one disputes his historical importance. Now Marx embalmed his thinking in the language of the Hegelian school. He founded it on a general philosophy of society which is known as the materialistic conception of history. Moreover, Marx put forth the claim that he had made socialism "scientific"—had shown that it was woven into the texture of natural phenomena. The Marxian paraphernalia crowds three heavy volumes, so elaborate and difficult that socialists rarely read them. I have known one socialist who lived leisurely on his country estate and claimed to have "looked" at every page of Marx. Most socialists, including the leaders, study selected passages and let it go at that. This is a wise economy based on a good instinct. For all the parade of learning and dialectic is an after-thought—an accident from the fact that the prophetic genius of Marx appeared in Germany under the incubus of Hegel. Marx saw what he wanted to do long before he wrote three volumes to justify it. Did not the Communist Manifesto appear many years before "Das Kapital"?

Nothing is more instructive than a socialist "experience" meeting at which everyone tries to tell how he came to be converted. These gatherings are notoriously untruthful—in fact, there is a genial pleasure in not telling the truth about one's salad days—in the socialist movement. The prevalent lie is to explain how the new convert, standing upon a mountain of facts, began to trace out the highways that led from hell to heaven. Everybody knows that no such process was actually lived through, and almost without exception the real story can be discerned: a man

[*175*]

was dissatisfied, he wanted a new condition of life, he embraced a theory that would justify his hopes and his discontent. For once you touch the biographies of human beings, the notion that political beliefs are logically determined collapses like a pricked balloon. In the language of philosophers, socialism as a living force is a product of the will—a will to beauty, order, neighborliness, not infrequently a will to health. Men desire first, then they reason; fascinated by the future, they invent a "scientific socialism" to get there.

Many people don't like to admit this. Or if they admit it, they do so with a sigh. Their minds construct a utopia—one in which all judgments are based on logical inference from syllogisms built on the law of mathematical probabilities. If you quote David Hume at them, and say that reason itself is an irrational impulse they think you are indulging in a silly paradox. I shall not pursue this point very far, but I believe it could be shown without too much difficulty that the rationalists are fascinated by a certain kind of thinking—logical and orderly thinking—and that it is their will to impose that method upon other men.

For fear that somebody may regard this as a play on words drawn from some ultra-modern "anti-intellectualist" source, let me quote Santayana. This is what the author of that masterly series "The Life of Reason" wrote in one of his earlier books: "The ideal of rationality is itself as arbitrary, as much dependent on the needs of a finite organization, as any other ideal. Only as ultimately securing tranquillity of mind, which the philosopher instinctively pursues, has it for him any necessity. In spite of the verbal propriety of saying that reason demands rationality, what really demands rationality, what makes it a good and indispensable thing and gives it all its authority, is not its own nature, but our need of it both in safe and economical action and in the pleasures of comprehension." Because rationality itself is a wilful exercise one hears Hymns to Reason and sees it personified as an extremely dignified goddess. For all the light and shadow of sentiment and passion play even about the syllogism.

The attempts of theorists to explain man's successes as rational acts and his failures as lapses of reason have always ended in a dismal and misty unreality. No genuine politician ever treats his constituents as reasoning animals. This is as true of the high politics of Isaiah as it is of the ward boss. Only the pathetic amateur deludes himself into thinking that, if he presents the major and minor premise, the voter will automatically draw the conclusion on election day. The successful politician—good or bad—deals with the dynamics—with the will, the hopes, the needs and the visions of men.

It isn't sentimentality which says that where there is no vision the people perisheth. Every time Tammany Hall sets off fireworks and oratory on the Fourth of July; every time the picture of Lincoln is displayed at a political convention; every red bandanna of the Progressives and red flag of the socialists; every song from "The Battle Hymn of the Republic" to the "International"; every metrical conclusion to a great speech—whether we stand at Armageddon, refuse to press upon the brow of labor another crown of thorns, or call upon the workers of the world to unite—every one of these slogans is an incitement of the will—an effort to energize politics. They are attempts to harness blind impulses to particular purposes. They are tributes to the sound practical sense of a vision in politics. No cause can succeed without them: so long as you rely on the efficacy of "scientific" demonstration and logical proof you can hold your conventions in anybody's back parlor and have room to spare.

I remember an observation that Lincoln Steffens made in a speech about Mayor Tom Johnson. "Tom failed," said Mr. Steffens, "because he was too practical." Coming from a man who had seen as much of actual politics as Mr. Steffens, it puzzled me a great deal. I taxed him with it later and he explained somewhat as follows: "Tom Johnson had a vision of Cleveland which he called The City on the Hill. He pictured the town emancipated from its ugliness and its cruelty—a beautiful city for free men and women. He used to talk of that vision to the 'cabinet' of political lieutenants which met every Sunday night at his house. He had all his appointees working for the City on the Hill. But when he went out campaigning before the people he talked only of three-cent fares and the tax outrages. Tom Johnson didn't show the people the City on the Hill. He didn't take them into his confidence. They never really saw what it was all about. And they went back on Tom Johnson."

That is one of Mr. Steffens's most acute observations. What makes it doubly interesting is that Tom Johnson confirmed it a few months before he died. His friends were telling him that his defeat was temporary, that the work he had begun was unchecked. It was plain that in the midst of his suffering, with death close by, he found great comfort in that assurance. But his mind was so realistic, his integrity so great that he could not blink the fact that there had been a defeat. Steffens was pointing out the explanation: "you did not show the people what you saw, you gave them the details, you fought their battles, you started to build, but you left them in darkness as to the final goal."

I wish I could recall the exact words in which Tom Johnson replied. For in them the greatest of the piecemeal reformers admitted the practical weakness of opportunist politics.

There is a type of radical who has an idea that he can insinuate advanced ideas into legislation without being caught. His plan of action is to keep his real program well concealed and to dole out sections of it to the public from time to time. John A. Hobson in "The Crisis of Liberalism" describes the "practical reformer" so that anybody can recognize him: "This revolt against ideas is carried so far that able men have come seriously to look upon progress as a matter for the manipulation of wire-pullers, something to be 'jobbed' in committee by sophistical notions or other clever trickery." Lincoln Steffens calls these people "our damned rascals." Mr. Hobson continues, "The attraction of some obvious gain, the suppression of some scandalous abuse of monopolist power by a private company, some needed enlargement of existing Municipal or State enterprise by lateral expansion—such are the sole springs of action." Well may Mr. Hobson inquire, *"Now, what provision is made for generating the motor power of progress in Collectivism?"*

No amount of architect's plans, bricks and mortar will build a house. Someone must have the wish to build it. So with the modern democratic state. Statesmanship cannot rest upon the good sense of its program. It must find popular feeling, organize it, and make that the motive power of government. If you study the success of Roosevelt the point is re-enforced. He is a man of will in whom millions of people have felt the embodiment of their own will. For a time Roosevelt was a man of destiny in the truest sense. He wanted what a nation wanted: his own power radiated power; he embodied a vision; Tom, Dick and Harry moved with his movement.

No use to deplore the fact. You cannot stop a living body with nothing at all. I think we may picture society as a compound of forces that are always changing. Put a vision in front of one of these currents and you can magnetize it in that direction. For visions alone organize popular passions. Try to ignore them or box them up, and they will burst forth destructively. When Haywood dramatizes the class struggle he uses class resentment for a social purpose. You may not like his purpose, but unless you can gather proletarian power into some better vision, you have no grounds for resenting Haywood. I fancy that the demonstration of King Canute settled once and for all the stupid attempt to ignore a moving force.

A dynamic conception of society always frightens a great number of people. It gives politics a restless and intractable quality. Pure reason is so gentlemanly, but will and the visions of a people—these are adventurous and incalculable forces. Most politicians living for the day prefer to ignore them. If only society will stand fairly still while their career is in the making they are content to avoid the actualities. But a politician with some imaginative interest in genuine affairs need not be seduced into the learned folly of pretending that reality is something else than it is. If he is to influence life he must deal with it. A deep respect is due the Schopenhauerian philosopher who looks upon the world, finds that its essence is evil, and turns towards insensitive calm. But no respect is due to anyone who sets out to reform the world by ignoring its quality. Whoever is bent upon shaping politics to better human uses must accept freely as his starting point the impulses that agitate human beings. If observation shows that reason is an instrument of will, then only confusion can result from pretending that it isn't.

I have called this misplaced "rationality" a piece of learned folly, because it shows itself most dangerously among those thinkers about politics who are divorced from action. In the Universities political movements are generally regarded as essentially static, cut and dried solids to be judged by their logical consistency. It is as if the stream of life had to be frozen before it could be studied. The socialist movement was given a certain amount of attention when I was an undergraduate. The discussion turned principally on two points: were rent, interest and dividends *earned*? Was collective ownership of capital a feasible scheme? And when the professor, who was a good dialectician, had proved that interest was a payment for service ("saving") and that public ownership was not practicable, it was assumed that socialism was disposed of. The passions, the needs, the hopes that generate this worldwide phenomenon were, I believe, pocketed and ignored under the pat saying: "Of course, socialism is not an economic policy, it's a religion." That was the end of the matter for the students of politics. It was then a matter for the divinity schools. If the same scholastic method is in force there, all that would be needed to crush socialism is to show its dogmatic inconsistencies.

The theorist is incompetent when he deals with socialism just because he assumes that men are determined by logic and that a false conclusion will stop a moving, creative force. Occasionally he recognizes the wilful character of politics: then he shakes his head, climbs into an ivory tower and deplores the moonshine, the religious manias and the passions of the mob. Real life is beyond his control and influence because real life is largely agitated by impulses and habits, unconscious needs, faith, hope and desire. With all his learning he is ineffective because, instead of trying to use the energies of men, he deplores them.

Suppose we recognize that creeds are instruments of the will, how would it alter the character of our thinking? Take an ancient quarrel like that over determinism. Whatever your philosophy, when you come to the test of actual facts you find, I think, all grades of freedom and determinism. For certain purposes you believe in free will, for others you do not. Thus, as Mr. Chesterton suggests, no determinist is prevented from saying "if you please" to the housemaid. In love, in your career, you have no doubt that "if" is a reality. But when you are engaged in scientific investigation, you try to reduce the spontaneous in life to a minimum. Mr. Arnold Bennett puts forth a rather curious hybrid when he advises us to treat ourselves as free agents and everyone else as an automaton. On the other hand Prof. Münsterberg has always insisted that in social relations we must always treat everyone as a purposeful, integrated character.

[*182*]

The Making of Creeds

Your doctrine, in short, depends on your purpose: a theory by itself is neither moral nor immoral, its value is conditioned by the purpose it serves. In any accurate sense theory is to be judged only as an effective or ineffective instrument of a desire: the discussion of doctrines is technical and not moral. A theory has no intrinsic value: that is why the devil can talk theology.

No creed possesses any final sanction. Human beings have desires that are far more important than the tools and toys and churches they make to satisfy them. It is more penetrating, in my opinion, to ask of a creed whether it served than whether it was "true." Try to judge the great beliefs that have swayed mankind by their inner logic or their empirical solidity and you stand forever, a dull pedant, apart from the interests of men. The Christian tradition did not survive because of Aquinas or fall before the Higher Criticism, nor will it be revived because someone proves the scientific plausibility of its doctrine. What we need to know about the Christian epic is the effect it had on men—true or false, they have believed in it for nineteen centuries. Where has it helped them, where hindered? What needs did it answer? What energies did it transmute? And what part of mankind did it neglect? Where did it begin to do violence to human nature?

Political creeds must receive the same treatment. The doctrine of the "social contract" formulated by Hobbes and made current by Rousseau can no longer be accepted as a true account of the origin of society. Jean-Jacques is in fact a supreme case—perhaps even a slight caricature—of the way in which formal creeds bolster up passionate wants. I quote from Prof. Walter's introduction in which he says that "The Social Contract *showed to those who were eager to be convinced* that no power was legitimate which was guilty of abuses. It is no wonder that its author was buried in the Pantheon with pompous procession, that the framers of the new Constitution, Thouret and Lièyes and La Fayette, did not forget and dared not forget its doctrines, that it was the textbook and the delight of Camille Desmoulins and Danton and St. Just, that Robespierre read it through once every day." In the perspective of history, no one feels that he has said the last word about a philosophy like Rousseau's after demonstrating its "untruth." Good or bad, it has meant too much for any such easy disposal. What shall we call an idea, objectively untrue, but practically of the highest importance?

The thinker who has faced this difficulty most radically is Georges Sorel in the "Reflexions sur la Violence." His doctrine of the "social myth" has seemed to many commentators one of those silly paradoxes that only a revolutionary syndicalist and Frenchman could have put forward. M. Sorel is engaged in presenting the General Strike as the decisive battle of the class struggle and the core of the socialist movement. Now whatever else he may be, M. Sorel is not naïve: the sharp criticism of other socialists was something he could not peacefully ignore. They told him that the General Strike was an idle dream, that it could never take place, that, even if it could, the results would not be very significant. Sidney Webb, in the customary Fabian fashion, had dismissed the General Strike as a sign of socialist immaturity. There is no doubt that M. Sorel felt the force of these attacks. But he was not ready to abandon his favorite idea because it had been shown to be unreasonable and impossible. Just the opposite effect showed itself and he seized the opportunity of turning an intellectual defeat into a spiritual triumph. This performance must have delighted him to the very bottom of his soul, for he has boasted that his task in life is to aid in ruining "le prestige de la culture bourgeoise."

M. Sorel's defence of the General Strike is very startling. He admits that it may never take place, that it is not a true picture of the goal of the socialist movement. Without a blush he informs us that this central gospel of the working class is simply a "myth." The admission frightens M. Sorel not at all. "It doesn't matter much," he remarks, "whether myths contain details actually destined to realization *in the scheme* of an historical future; they are not astrological almanacks; it may even be that nothing of what they express will actually happen—as in the case of that catastrophe which the early Christians expected. Are we not accustomed in daily life to recognizing that the reality differs very greatly from the ideas of it that we made before we acted? Yet that doesn't hinder us from making resolutions. . . . Myths must be judged as instruments for acting upon present conditions; all discussion about the manner of applying them concretely to the course of history is senseless. *The entire myth is what counts*. . . . There is no use then in reasoning about details which might arise in the midst of the class struggle . . . even though the revolutionists should be deceiving themselves through and through in making a fantastic picture of the general strike, this picture would still have been a power of the highest order in preparing for revolution, so long as it expressed completely all the aspirations of socialism and bound together revolutionary ideas with a precision and firmness that no other methods of thought could have given."

It may well be imagined that this highly sophisticated doctrine was regarded as perverse. All the ordinary prejudices of thought are irritated by a thinker who frankly advises masses of his fellow-men to hold fast to a belief which by all the canons of common sense is nothing but an illusion. M. Sorel must have felt the need of closer statement, for in a letter to Daniel Halèvy, published in the second edition, he makes his position much clearer. "Revolutionary myths . . ." we read, "enable us to understand the activity, the feelings, and the ideas of a populace preparing to enter into a decisive struggle; *they are not descriptions of things, but expressions of will.*" The italics are mine: they set in relief the insight that makes M. Sorel so important to our discussion. I do not know whether a quotation torn from its context can possibly do justice to its author. I do know that for any real grasp of this point it is necessary to read M. Sorel with great sympathy.

One must grant at least that he has made an accurate observation. The history of the world is full of great myths which have had the most concrete results. M. Sorel cites primitive Christianity, the Reformation, the French Revolution and the Mazzini campaign. The men who took part in those great social movements summed up their aspiration in pictures of decisive battles resulting in the ultimate triumph of their cause. We in America might add an example from our own political life. For it is Theodore Roosevelt who is actually attempting to make himself and his admirers the heroes of a new social myth. Did he not announce from the platform at Chicago—"we stand at Armageddon and we battle for the Lord"?

Let no one dismiss M. Sorel then as an empty paradoxer. The myth is not one of the outgrown crudities of our pagan ancestors. We, in the midst of our science and our rationalism, are still making myths, and their force is felt in the actual affairs of life. They convey an impulse, not a program, nor a plan of reconstruction. Their practical value cannot be ignored, for they embody the motor currents in social life.

Myths are to be judged, as M. Sorel says, by their ability to express aspiration. They stand or fall by that. In such a test the Christian myth, for example, would be valued for its power of incarnating human desire. That it did not do so completely is the cause of its decline. From Aucassin to Nietzsche men have resented it as a partial and stunting dream. It had too little room, for profane love, and only by turning the Church of Christ into the Church Militant could the essential Christian passivity obtain the assent of aggressive and masculine races. To-day traditional Christianity has weakened in the face of man's interest in the conquest of this world. The liberal and advanced churches recognize this fact by exhibiting a great preoccupation with everyday affairs. Now they may be doing important service—I have no wish to deny that—but when the Christian Churches turn to civics, to reformism or socialism, they are in fact announcing that the Christian dream is dead. They may continue to practice some of its moral teachings and hold to some of its creed, but the Christian impulse is for them no longer active. A new dream, which they reverently call Christian, has sprung from their desires.

During their life these social myths contain a nation's finest energy. It is just because they are "not descriptions of things, but expressions of will" that their influence is so great. Ignore what a man desires and you ignore the very source of his power; run against the grain of a nation's genius and see where you get with your laws. Robert Burns was right when he preferred poetry to charters. The recognition of this truth by Sorel is one of the most impressive events in the revolutionary movement. Standing as a spokesman of an actual social revolt, he has not lost his vision because he understands its function. If Machiavelli is a symbol of the political theorist making reason an instrument of purpose, we may take Sorel as a self-conscious representative of the impulses which generate purpose.

It must not be supposed that respect for the myth is a discovery of Sorel's. He is but one of a number of contemporary thinkers who have reacted against a very stupid prejudice of nineteenth-century science to the effect that the mental habits of human beings were not "facts." Unless ideas mirrored external nature they were regarded as beneath the notice of the scientific mind. But in more recent years we have come to realize that, in a world so full of ignorance and mistake, error itself is worthy of study. Our untrue ideas are significant because they influence our lives enormously. They are "facts" to be investigated. One might point to the great illumination that has resulted from Freud's analysis of the abracadabra of our dreams. No one can any longer dismiss the fantasy because it is logically inconsistent, superficilly absurd, or objectively untrue. William James might also be cited for his defense of those beliefs that are beyond the realm of proof. His essay, "The Will to Believe," is a declaration of independence, which says in effect that scientific demonstration is not the only test of ideas. He stated the case for those beliefs which influence life so deeply, though they fail to describe it. James himself was very disconcerting to many scientists because he insisted on expressing his aspirations about the universe in what his colleague Santayana calls a "romantic cosmology": "I am far from wishing to suggest that such a view seems to me more probable than conventional idealism or the Christian Orthodoxy. All three are in the region of dramatic system-making and myth, to which probabilities are irrelevant."

It is impossible to leave this point without quoting Nietzsche, who had this insight and stated it most provocatively. In "Beyond Good and Evil" Nietzsche says flatly that "the falseness of an opinion is not for us any objection to it: it is here, perhaps, that our new language sounds most strangely. The question is, how far an opinion is life-furthering, life-preserving, species-preserving, perhaps species-rearing. . . ." Then he comments on the philosophers. "They all pose as though their real opinions had been discovered and attained through the self-evolving of a cold, pure, divinely indifferent dialectic . . . ; whereas, in fact, a prejudiced proposition, idea, or 'suggestion,' which is generally their heart's desire abstracted and refined, is defended by them with arguments sought out after the event. They are all advocates who do not wish to be regarded as such, generally astute defenders, also, of their prejudices, which they dub 'truths'—and *very* far from having the conscience which bravely admits this to itself; very far from having the good taste or the courage which goes so far as to let this be understood, perhaps to warn friend or foe, or in cheerful confidence and self-ridicule. . . . It has gradually become clear to me what every great philosophy up till now has consisted of—namely, the confession of its originator, and a species of involuntary and unconscious autobiography, and, moreover, that the moral (or immoral) purpose in every philosophy has constituted the true vital germ out of which the entire plant has always grown. . . . Whoever considers the fundamental impulses of man with a view to determining how far they may have acted as *inspiring* genii (or as demons and cobolds) will find that they have all practiced philosophy at one time or another, and that each one of them would have been only too glad to look upon itself as the ultimate end of existence and the legitimate *lord* over all the other innpulses. For every impulse is imperious, and, as *such*, attempts to philosophize."

What Nietzsche has done here is, in his swash-buckling fashion, to cut under the abstract and final pretensions of creeds. Difficulties arise when we try to apply this wisdom in the present. That dogmas *were* instruments of human purposes is not so incredible; that they still *are* instruments is not so clear to everyone; and that they will be, that they should be—this seems a monstrous attack on the citadel of truth. It is possible to believe that other men's theories were temporary and merely useful; we like to believe that ours will have a greater authority.

The Making of Creeds

It seems like topsy-turvyland to make reason serve the irrational. Yet that is just what it has always done, and ought always to do. Many of us are ready to grant that in the past men's motives were deeper than their intellects: we forgive them with a kind of self-righteousness which says that they knew not what they did. But to follow the great tradition of human wisdom deliberately, with our eyes open in the manner of Sorel, that seems a crazy procedure. A notion of intellectual honor fights against it: we think we must aim at final truth, and not allow autobiography to creep into speculation.

Now the trouble with such an idol is that autobiography creeps in anyway. The more we censor it, the more likely it is to appear disguised, to fool us subtly and perhaps dangerously. The men like Nietzsche and James who show the wilful origin of creeds are in reality the best watchers of the citadel of truth. For there is nothing disastrous in the temporary nature of our ideas. They are always that. But there may very easily be a train of evil in the self-deception which regards them as final. I think God will forgive us our skepticism sooner than our Inquisitions.

From the political point of view, another observation is necessary. The creed of a Rousseau, for example, is active in politics, not for what it says, but for what people think it says. I have urged that Marx found scientific reasons for what he wanted to do. It is important to add that the people who adopted his reasons for what they wanted to do were not any too respectful of Marx's reasons. Thus the so-called materialistic philosophy of Karl Marx is not by any means identical with the theories one hears among Marxian socialists. There is a big distortion in the transmitting of ideas. A common purpose, far more than common ideas, binds Marx to his followers. And when a man comes to write about his philosophy he is confronted with a choice: shall the creed described be that of Marx or of the Marxians?

For the study of politics I should say unhesitatingly that it is more important to know what socialist leaders, stump speakers, pamphleteers, think Marx meant, than to know what he said. For then you are dealing with living ideas: to search his text has its uses, but compared with the actual tradition of Marx it is the work of pedantry. I say this here for two reasons—because I hope to avoid the critical attack of the genuine Marxian specialist, and because the observation is, I believe, relevant to our subject.

Relevant it is in that it suggests the importance of style, of propaganda, the popularization of ideas. The host of men who stand between a great thinker and the average man are not automatic transmitters. They work on the ideas; perhaps that is why a genius usually hates his disciples. It is interesting to notice the explanation given by Frau Förster-Nietzsche for her brother's quarrel with Wagner. She dates it from the time when Nietzsche, under the guise of Wagnerian propaganda, began to expound himself. The critics and interpreters are themselves creative. It is really unfair to speak of the Marxian philosophy as a political force. It is juster to speak of the Marxian tradition.

So when I write of Marx's influence I have in mind what men and women in socialist meetings, in daily life here in America, hold as a faith and attribute to Marx. There is no pretension whatever to any critical study of "Das Kapital" itself. I am thinking rather of stuffy halls in which an earnest voice is expounding "the evolution of capitalism," of little groups, curious and bewildered, listening in the streets of New York to the story of the battle between the "master class" and the "working class," of little red pamphlets, of newspapers, and cartoons—awkward, badly printed and not very genial, a great stream of spellbinding and controversy through which the aspirations of millions are becoming articulate:

The tradition is saying that "the system" and not the individual is at fault. It describes that system as one in which a small class owns the means of production and holds the rest of mankind in bondage. Arts, religions, laws, as well as vice and crime and degradation, have their source in this central economic condition. If you want to understand our life you must see that it is determined by the massing of capital in the hands of a few. All epochs are determined by economic arrangements. But a system of property always contains within itself "the seeds of its own destruction." Mechanical inventions suggest a change: a dispossessed class compels it. So mankind has progressed through savagery, chattel slavery, serfdom, to "wage slavery" or the capitalism of to-day. This age is pregnant with the socialism of to-morrow.

So roughly the tradition is handed on. Two sets of idea seem to dominate it: we are creatures of economic conditions; a war of classes is being fought everywhere in which the proletariat will ultimately capture the industrial machinery and produce a sound economic life as the basis of peace and happiness for all. The emphasis on environment is insistent. Facts are marshaled, the news of the day is interpreted to show that men are determined by economic conditions. This fixation has brought down upon the socialists a torrent of abuse in which "atheism" and "materialism" are prevailing epithets. But the propaganda continues and the philosophy spreads, penetrating reform groups, social workers, historians, and sociologists.

It has served the socialist purpose well. To the workingmen it has brought home the importance of capturing the control of industry. Economic determinism has been an antidote to mere preaching of goodness, to hero-worship and political quackery. Socialism to succeed had to concentrate attention on the ownership of capital: whenever any other interest like religion or patriotism threatened to diffuse that attention, socialist leaders have always been ready to show that the economic fact is more central. Dignity and prestige were supplied by making economics the key of history; passion was chained by building paradise upon it.

In all the political philosophies there is none so adapted to its end. Every sanction that mankind respects has been grouped about this one purpose—the control of capital. It is as if all history converged upon the issue, and the workers in the cause feel that they carry within them the destiny of the race. Start anywhere with an orthodox socialist and he will lead you to this supreme economic situation. Tyrannies and race hatred, national rivalries, sex problems, the difficulties of artistic endeavor, all failures, crimes, vices—there is not one which he will not relate to private capitalism. Nor is there anything disingenuous about this focusing of the attention: a real belief is there. Of course you will find plenty of socialists who see other issues and who smile a bit at the rigors of economic determinism. In these later days there is, in fact, a decided loosening in the creed. But it is fair to say that the mass of socialists hold this philosophy with as much solemnity as a reformer held his when he wrote to me that the cure for obscenity was the taxation of land values and absolute free trade.

Singlemindedness has done good service. It has bound the world together and has helped men to think socially. Turning their attention away from the romanticism of history, the materialistic philosophy has helped them to look at realities. It has engendered a fine conern about average people, about the voiceless multitudes who have been left to pass unnoticed. Not least among the blessings is a shattering of the good-and-bad-man theory: the assassination of tyrants or the adoration of saviors. A shallow and specious other-worldliness has been driven out; an other-worldliness which is really nothing but laziness about this one. And if from a speculative angle the Marxian tradition has shaded too heavily the economic facts, it was at least a plausible and practical exaggeration.

But the drawbacks are becoming more and more evident as socialism approaches nearer to power and responsibility. The feeling that man is a creature and not a creator is disastrous as a personal creed when you come to act. If you insist upon being "determined by conditions" you do hesitate about saying "I shall." You are likely to wait for something to determine you. Personal initiative and individual genius are poorly regarded: many socialists are suspicious of originality. This philosophy, so useful in propaganda, is becoming a burden in action. That is another way of saying that the instrument has turned into an idol.

[*195*]

For while it is illuminating to see how environment moulds men, it is absolutely essential that men regard themselves as moulders of their environment. A new philosophical basis is becoming increasingly necessary to socialism —one that may not be "truer" than the old materialism but that shall simply be more useful. Having learned for a long time what is done to us, we are now faced with the task of doing. With this changed purpose goes a change of instruments. All over the world socialists are breaking away from the stultifying influence of the outworn determinism. For the time is at hand when they must cease to look upon socialism as inevitable in order to make it so.

Nor will the philosophy of class warfare serve this new need. That can be effective only so long as the working-class is without sovereignty. But no sooner has it achieved power than a new outlook is needed in order to know what to do with it. The tactics of the battlefield are of no use when the battle is won.

I picture this philosophy as one of deliberate choices. The underlying tone of it is that society is made by man for man's uses, that reforms are inventions to be applied when by experiment they show their civilizing value. Emphasis is placed upon the devising, adapting, constructing faculties. There is no reason to believe that this view is any colder than that of the war of class against class. It will generate no less energy. Men to-day can feel almost as much zest in the building of the Panama Canal as they did in a military victory. Their domineering impulses find satisfaction in conquering things, in subjecting brute forces to human purposes. This sense of mastery in a winning battle against the conditions of our life is, I believe, the social myth that will inspire our reconstructions. We shall feel free to choose among alternatives—to take this much of socialism, insert so much syndicalism, leave standing what of capitalism seems worth conserving. We shall be making own house for our own needs, cities to suit ourselves, and we shall, believe ourselves capable of moving mountains, as engineers do, when mountains stand in their way.

And history, science, philosophy will support our hopes. What will fascinate us in the past will be the records of inventions, of great choices, of those alternatives on which destiny seems to hang. The splendid epochs will be interpreted as monuments of man's creation, not of his propulsion. We shall be interested primarily in the way nations established their civilization in spite of hostile conditions. Admiration will go out to the men who did not submit, who bent things to human use. We may see the entire tragedy of life in being driven.

Half-truths and illusions, if you like, but tonic. This view will suit our mood. For we shall be making and the makers of history will become more real to us. Instead of urging that issues are inevitable, instead of being swamped by problems that are unavoidable, we may stand up and affirm the issues we propose to handle. Perhaps we shall say with Nietzsche:

"Let the value of everything be dete mined afresh by you."

CHAPTER VIII

THE RED HERRING

A T the beginning of every campaign the newspapers
tell about secret conferences in which the candidate
and his managers decide upon "the line of attack." The
approach to issues, the way in which they shall be stressed,
what shall be put forward in one part of the country and what
in another, are discussed at these meetings. Here is where the
real program of a party is worked out. The document produced at the convention is at its best nothing but a suggestive formality. It is not until the speakers and the publicity
agents have actually begun to animate it that the country sees
what the party is about. It is as if the convention adopted the
Decalogue, while these secret conferences decided which of
the Commandments was to be made the issue. Almost
always, of course, the decision is entirely a "practical" one,
which means that each section of people is exhorted to practice the commandment it likes the most. Thus for the bur-
glars is selected, not the eighth tablet, but the one on which
is recommended a day of rest from labor; to the happily married is preached the seventh commandment.

These conferences are decisive. On them depends the
educational value of a campaign, and the men who partici-

pate in them, being in a position to state the issues and point them, determine the political interests of the people for a considerable period of time. To-day in America, for example, no candidate can escape entirely that underlying irritation which socialists call poverty and some call the high cost of living. But the conspicuous candidates do decide what direction thought shall take about this condition. They can center it upon the tariff or the trusts or even the currency.

Thus Mr. Roosevelt has always had a remarkable power of diverting the country from the tariff to the control of the trusts. His Democratic opponents, especially Woodrow Wilson, are, as I write, in the midst of the Presidential campaign of 1912, trying to focus attention on the tariff. In a way the battle resembles a tug-of-war in which each of the two leading candidates is trying to pull the nation over to his favorite issue. On the side you can see the Prohibitionists endeavoring to make the country see drink as a central problem; the emerging socialists insisting that not the tariff, or liquor, or the control of trusts, but the ownership of capital should be the heart of the discussion. Electoral campaigns do not resemble debates so much as they do competing amusement shows where, with bright lights, gaudy posters and persuasive, insistent voices, each booth is trying to collect a crowd. The victory in a campaign is far more likely to go to the most plausible diagnosis than to the most convincing method of cure. Once a party can induce the country to see its issue as supreme the greater part of its task is done.

The clever choice of issues influences all politics from the petty manœuvers of a ward leader to the most brilliant creative statesmanship. I remember an instance that happened at the beginning of the first socialist administration in Schenectady: The officials had out of the goodness of their hearts suspended a city ordinance which forbade coasting with bob-sleds on the hills of the city. A few days later one of the sleds ran into a wagon and a little girl was killed. The opposition papers put the accident into scareheads with the result that public opinion became very bitter. It looked like a bad crisis at the very beginning and the old ring politicians made the most of it. But they had reckoned without the political shrewdness of the socialists. For in the second day of excitement, the mayor made public a plan by which the main business street of the town was to be lighted with high-power lamps and turned into a "brilliant white way of Schenectady." The swiftness with which the papers displaced the gruesome details of the little girl's death by exultation over the business future of the city was a caution. Public attention was shifted and a political crisis avoided. I tell this story simply as a suggestive fact. The ethical considerations do not concern us here.

There is nothing exceptional about the case. Whenever governments enter upon foreign invasions in order to avoid civil wars, the same trick is practiced. In the Southern States the race issue has been thrust forward persistently to prevent an economic alignment. Thus you hear from Southerners that unless socialism gives up its demand for racial equality, the propaganda cannot go forward. How often in great strikes have riots been started in order to prevent the public from listening, to the workers' demands! It is an old story—the red herring dragged across the path in order to destroy the scent.

A Preface to Politics

Having seen the evil results we have come to detest a conscious choice of issues, to feel that it smacks of sinister plotting. The vile practice of yellow newspapers and chauvinistic politicians is almost the only experience of it we have. Religion, patriotism, race, and sex are the favorite red herrings of foul political method—they are the most successful because they explode so easily and flood the mind with those unconscious prejudices which make critical thinking difficult. Yet for all its abuse the deliberate choice of issues is one of the high selective arts of the statesman. In the debased form we know it there is little encouragement. But the devil is merely a fallen angel, and when God lost Satan he lost one of his best lieutenants. It is always a pretty good working rule that whatever is a great power of evil may become a great power for good. Certainly nothing so effective in the art of politics can be left out of the equipment of the statesman.

Looked at closely, the deliberate making of issues is very nearly the core of the statesman's task. His greatest wisdom is required to select a policy that will fertilize the public mind. He fails when the issue he sets is sterile; he is incompetent if the issue does not lead to the human center of a problem; whenever the statesman allows the voters to trifle with taboos and by-products, to wander into blind alleys like "16 to 1," his leadership is a public calamity. The newspaper or politician which tries to make an issue out of a supposed "prosperity" or out of admiration for the mere successes of our ancestors is doing its best to choke off the creative energies in politics. All the stultification of the stand-pat mind may be described as inability, and perhaps unwillingness, to nourish a fruitful choice of issues.

The Red Herring

That choice is altogether too limited in America, anyway. Political discussion, whether reactionary or radical, is monotonously confined to very few issues. It is as if social life were prevented from irrigating political thought. A subject like the tariff, for example, has absorbed an amount of attention which would justify an historian in calling it the incubus of American politics. Now the exaltation of one issue like that is obviously out of all proportion to its significance. A contributory factor it certainly is, but the country's destiny is not bound up finally with its solution. The everlasting reiterations about the tariff take up altogether too much time. To any government that was clear about values, that saw all problems in their relation to human life, the tariff would be an incident, a mechanical device and little else. High protectionist and free trader alike fall under the indictment—for a tariff wall is neither so high as heaven nor so broad as the earth. It may be necessary to have dykes on portions of the seashore; they may be superfluous elsewhere. But to concentrate nine-tenths of your attention on the subject of dykes is to forget the civilization they are supposed to protect. A wall is a wall: the presence of it will not do the work of civilization—the absence of it does not absolve anyone from the tasks of social life. That a statecraft might deal with the tariff as an aid to its purposes is evident. But anyone who makes the tariff the principal concern of statecraft is, I believe, mistaking the hedge for the house.

The tariff controversy is almost as old as the nation. A more recent one is what Senator La Follette calls "The great issue before the American people to-day, . . . the control of their own government." It has taken the form of an attack on corruption, on what is vaguely called "special privilege" and of a demand for a certain amount of political machinery such as direct primaries, the initiative, referendum, and recall. The agitation has a curious sterility: the people are exhorted to control their own government, but they are given very little advice as to what they are to do with it when they control it. Of course, the leaders who spend so much time demanding these mechanical changes undoubtedly see them as a safeguard against corrupt politicians and what Roosevelt calls "their respectable allies and figureheads, who have ruled and legislated and decided as if in some way the vested rights of privilege had a first mortgage on the whole United States." But look at the *way* these inovations are presented and I think the feeling is unavoidable that the control of government is emphasized as an end in itself. Now an observation of this kind is immediately open to dispute: it is not a clear-cut distinction but a rather subtle matter of stress—an impression rather than a definite conviction.

Yet when you look at the career of Judge Lindsey in Denver the impression is sharpened by contrast. What gave his exposure of corruption a peculiar vitality was that it rested on a very positive human ideal: the happiness of children in a big city. Lindsey's attack on vice and financial jobbery was perhaps the most convincing piece of muckraking ever done in this country for the very reason that it sprang from a concern about real human beings instead of abstractions about democracy or righteousness. From the point of view of the political hack, Judge Lindsey made a most distressing use of the red herring. He brought the happiness of childhood into political discussion, and this opened up a new source of political power. By touching something deeply instinctive in millions of people, Judge Lindsey animated dull proposals with human interest. The pettifogging objections to some social plan had very little chance of survival owing to the dynamic power of the reformers. It was an excellent example of the creative results that come from centering a political problem on human nature.

If you move only from legality to legality, you halt and hesitate, each step is a monstrous task. If the reformer is a pure opportunist, and lays out only "the next step," that step will be very difficult. But if he aims at some real human end, at the genuine concerns of men, women, and children, if he can make the democracy see and feel that end, the little mechanical devices of suffrage and primaries and tariffs will be dealt with as a craftsman deals with his tools. But to say that we must make tools first, and then begin, is to invert the process of life. Men did not agree to refrain from travel until a railroad was built. To make the manufacture of instruments an ideal is to lose much of their ideal value. A nation bent upon a policy of social invention would make its tools an incident. But just this perception is lacking in many propagandists. That is why their issues are so sterile; that is why the absorption in "next steps" is a diversion from statesmanship.

The narrowness of American political issues is a fixation upon instruments. Tradition has centered upon the tariff, the trusts, the currency, and electoral machinery as the items of consideration. It is the failure to go behind them —to see them as the pale servants of a vivid social life— that keeps our politics in bondage to a few problems. It is a common experience repeated in you and me. Once our profession becomes all absorbing it hardens into pedantry. "A human being," says Wells, "who is a philosopher in the first place, a teacher in the first place, or a statesman in the first place is thereby and inevitably, though he bring God-like gifts to the pretense—a quack."

Reformers particularly resent the enlargement of political issues. I have heard socialists denounce other socialists for occupying themselves with the problems of sex. The claim was that these questions should be put aside so as not to disturb the immediate program. The socialists knew from experience that sex views cut across economic ones—that a new interest breaks up the alignment. Woodrow Wilson expressed this same fear in his views on the liquor question: after declaring for local option he went on to say that "the questions involved are social and moral and are not susceptible of being made part of a party program. Whenever they have been made the subject matter of party contests they have cut the lines of party organization and party action athwart, to the utter confusion of political action in every other field. . . . I do not believe party programs of the highest consequence to the political life of the State and of the nation ought to be thrust on one side and hopelessly embarrassed for long periods together by making a political issue of a great question which is essentially non-political, non-partisan, moral and social in its nature."

That statement was issued at the beginning of a campaign in which Woodrow Wilson was the nominee of a party that has always been closely associated with the liquor interests. The bogey of the saloon had presented itself early:

it was very clear that an affirmative position by the candidate was sure to alienate either the temperance or the "liquor vote." No doubt a sense of this dilemma is partly responsible for Wilson's earnest plea that the question of liquor be left out of the campaign. He saw the confusion and embarrassment he speaks of as an immediate danger. Like his views on immigration and Chinese labor it was a red herring across his path. It would, if brought into prominence, cut the lines of party action athwart.

His theoretical grounds for ignoring the question in politics are very interesting just because they are vitalized by this practical difficulty which he faced. Like all party men Woodrow Wilson had thrust upon him here a danger that haunts every political program. The more issues a party meets the less votes it is likely to poll. And for a very simple reason: you cannot keep the citizenship of a nation like this bound in its allegiance to two large parties unless you make the grounds of allegiance very simple and very obvious. If you are to hold five or six million voters enlisted under one emblem the less specific you are and the fewer issues you raise the more probable it is that you can stop this host from quarreling within the ranks.

No doubt this is a partial explanation of the bareness of American politics. The two big parties have had to preserve a superficial homogeneity; and a platitude is more potent than an issue. The minor parties—Populist, Prohibition, Independence League and Socialist—have shown a much greater willingness to face new problems. Their view of national policy has always been more inclusive, perhaps for the very reason that their membership is so much more exclusive. But if anyone wishes a smashing illustration of this paradox let him consider the rapid progress of Roosevelt's philosophy in the very short time between the Republican Convention in June to the Progressive Convention in August, 1912. As soon as Roosevelt had thrown off the burden of preserving a false harmony among irreconcilable Republicans, he issued a platform full of definiteness and square dealing with many issues. He was talking to a minority party. But Roosevelt's genius is not that of group leadership. He longs for majorities. He set out to make the campaign a battle between the Progressives and the Democrats—the old discredited Republicans fell back into a rather dead conservative minority. No sooner did Roosevelt take the stump than the paradox loomed up before him. His speeches began to turn on platitudes—on the vague idealism and indisputable moralities of the Decalogue and the Sermon on the Mount. The fearlessness of the Chicago confession was melted down into a featureless alloy.

The embarrassment from the liquor question which Woodrow Wilson feared does not arise because teetotaler and drunkard both become intoxicated when they discuss the saloon. It would come just as much from a radical program of land taxation, factory reform, or trust control. Let anyone of these issues be injected into his campaign and the lines of party action would be cut "athwart." For Woodrow Wilson was dealing with the inevitable embarrassment of a party system dependent on an inexpressive homogeneity. The grouping of the voters into two large herds costs a large price: it means that issues must be so simplified and selected that the real demands of the nation rise only now and then to the level of political discussion. The more people a party contains the less it expresses their needs.

Woodrow Wilson's diagnosis of the red herring in politics is obviously correct. A new issue does embarrass a wholesale organization of the voters. His desire to avoid it in the midst of a campaign is understandable. His urgent plea that the liquor question be kept a local issue may be wise. But the general philosophy which says that the party system should not be cut athwart is at least open to serious dispute. Instead of an evil, it looks to me like progress towards greater responsivenss of parties to popular need. It is good to disturb alignments: to break up a superficial unanimity. The masses of people held together under the name Democratic are bound in an enervating communion. The real groups dare not speak their convictions for fear the crust will break. It is as if you had thrown a large sheet over a mass of men and made them anonymous.

The man who raises new issues has always been distasteful to politicians. He musses up what had been so tidily arranged. I remember once speaking to a local boss about woman suffrage. His objections were very simple: "We've got the organization in fine shape now—we know where every voter in the district stands. But you let all the women vote and we'll be confused as the devil. It'll be an awful job keeping track of them." He felt what many a manufacturer feels when somebody has the impertinence to invent a process which disturbs the routine of business.

Hard as it is upon the immediate plans of the politican, it is a national blessing when the lines of party action are cut athwart by new issues. I recognize that the red herring is more often frivolous and personal—a matter of misrepresentation and spite—than an honest attempt to enlarge the scope of politics. However, a fine thing must not be deplored because it is open to vicious caricature. To the party worker the petty and the honest issue are equally disturbing. The break-up of the parties into expressive groups would be a ventilation of our national life. No use to cry peace when there is no peace. The false bonds are best broken: with their collapse would come a release of social energy into political discussion. For every country is a mass of minorities which should find a voice in public affairs. Any device like proportional representation and preferential voting which facilitates the political expression of group interests is worth having. The objection that popular government cannot be conducted without the two party system is, I believe, refuted by the experience of Europe. If I had to choose between a Congressional caucus and a coalition ministry, I should not have to hesitate very long. But no one need go abroad for actual experience: in the United States Senate during the Taft administration there were really three parties—Republicans, Insurgents and Democrats. Public business went ahead with at least as much effectiveness as under the old Aldrich ring.

There are deeper reasons for urging a breakup of herd-politics. It is not only desirable that groups should be able to contribute to public discussion: it is absolutely essential if the parliamentary method is not to be superseded by direct and violent action. The two party system chokes off the cry of a minority—perhaps the best way there is of precipitating an explosion. An Englishman once told me that the utter freedom of speech in Hyde Park was the best safe-guard England had against the doctrines that were pro-pounded there. An anarchist who was invited to address Congress would be a mild person compared to the man forbidden to speak in the streets of San Diego. For many a bomb has exploded into rhetoric.

The rigidity of the two-party system is, I believe, disastrous: it ignores issues without settling them, dulls and wastes the energies of active groups, and chokes off the protests which should find a civilized expression in public life. A recognition of what an incubus it is should make us hospitable to all those devices which aim at making politics responsive by disturbing the alignments of habit. The initiative and referendum will help: they are a method of voting on definite issues instead of electing an administration in bulk. If cleverly handled these electoral devices should act as a check on a wholesale attitude toward politics. Men could agree on a candidate and disagree on a measure. Another device is the separation of municipal, state and national elections: to hold them all at the same time is an inducement to prevent the voter from splitting his allegiance. Proportional representation and preferential voting I have mentioned. The short ballot is a psychological principle which must be taken into account wherever there is voting: it will help the differentiation of political groups by concentrating the attention on essential choices. The recall of public officials is in part a policeman's club, in part a clumsy way of getting around the American prejudice for a fixed term of office. That rigidity which by the mere movement of the calendar throws an official out of office in the midst of his work or compels him to go campaigning is merely the crude method of a democracy without confidence in itself. The recall is a half-hearted and negative way of dealing with this difficulty. It does enable us to rid ourselves of an officer we don't like instead of having to wait until the earth has revolved to a certain place about the sun. But we still have to vote on a fixed date whether we have anything to vote upon or not. If a recall election is held when the people petition for it, why not all elections?

In ways like these we shall go on inventing methods by which the fictitious party alignments can be dissolved. There is one device suggested now and then, tried, I believe, in a few places, and vaguely championed by some socialists. It is called in German an "Interessenvertrag"—a political representation by trade interests as well as by geographical districts. Perhaps this is the direction towards which the bi-cameral legislature will develop. One chamber would then represent a man's sectional interests as a consumer: the other his professional interests as a producer. The railway workers, the miners, the doctors, the teachers, the retail merchants would have direct representation in the "Interessenvertrag." You might call it a Chamber of Special Interests. I know how that phrase "Special Interests" hurts. In popular usage we apply it only to corrupting businesses. But our feeling against them should not blind us to the fact that every group in the community has its special interests. They will always exist until mankind becomes a homogeneous jelly. The problem is to find some social adjustment for all the special interests of a nation. That is best achieved by open recognition and clear representation. Let no one then confuse the "Interessenvertrag" with those existing legislatures which are secret Chambers of Special Privilege.

The scheme is worth looking at for it does do away with the present dilemma of the citizen in which he wonders helplessly whether he ought to vote as a consumer or as a producer. I believe he should have both votes, and the "Interessenvertrag" is a way.

These devices are mentioned here as illustrations and not as conclusions. You can think of them as arrangements by which the red herring is turned from a pest into a benefit. I grant that in the rigid political conditions prevailing to-day a new issue is an embarrassment, perhaps a hindrance to the procedure of political life. But instead of narrowing the scope of politics, to avoid it, the only sensible thing to do is to invent methods which will allow needs and problems and group interests avenues into politics.

But a suggestion like this is sure to be met with the argument which Woodrow Wilson has in mind when he says that the "questions involved are social and moral and are not susceptible of being made parts of a party program." He voices a common belief when he insists that there are moral and social problems, "essentially nonpolitical." Innocent as it looks at first sight this plea by Woodrow Wilson is weighted with the tradition of a century and a half. To my mind it symbolizes a view of the state which we are outgrowing, and throws into relief the view towards which we are struggling. Its implications are well worth tracing, for through them I think we can come to understand better the method of Twentieth Century politics.

It is perfectly true that that government is best which

governs least. It is equally true that that government is best which provides most. The first truth belongs to the Eighteenth Century: the second to the Twentieth. Neither of them can be neglected in our attitude towards the state. Without the Jeffersonian distrust of the police we might easily grow into an impertinent and tyrannous collectivism: without a vivid sense of the possibilities of the state we abandon the supreme instrument of civilization. The two theories need to be held together, yet clearly distinguished.

Government has been an exalted policeman: it was there to guard property and to prevent us from quarreling too violently. That was about all it was good for. Yet society found problems on its hands—problems which Woodrow Wilson calls moral and social in their nature. Vice and crime, disease, and grinding poverty forced themselves on the attention of the community. A typical example is the way the social evil compelled the city of Chicago to begin an investigation. Yet when government was asked to handle the question it had for wisdom an ancient conception of itself as a policeman. Its only method was to forbid, to prosecute, to jail—in short, to use the taboo. But experience has shown that the taboo will not solve "moral and social questions"—that nine times out of ten it aggravates the disease. Political action becomes a petty, futile, mean little intrusion when its only method is prosecution.

No wonder then that conservatively-minded men pray that moral and social questions be kept out of politics; no wonder that more daring souls begin to hate the whole idea of government and take to anarchism. So long as the state is conceived merely as an agent of repression, the less it interferes with our lives, the better. Much of the horror of socialism comes from a belief that by increasing the functions of government its regulating power over our daily lives will grow into a tyranny. I share this horror when certain socialists begin to propound their schemes. There is a dreadful amount of forcible scrubbing and arranging and pocketing implied in some socialisms. There is a wish to have the state use its position as general employer to become a censor of morals and arbiter of elegance, like the benevolent employers of the day who take an impertinent interest in the private lives of their workers. Without any doubt socialism has within it the germs of that great bureaucratic tyranny which Chesterton and Belloc have named the Servile State.

So it is a wise instinct that makes men jealous of the policeman's power. Far better we may say that moral and social problems be left to private solution than that they be subjected to the clumsy method of the taboo. When Woodrow Wilson argues that social problems are not susceptible to treatment in a party program, he must mean only one thing: that they cannot be handled by the state as he conceives it. He is right. His attitude is far better than that of the Vice Commission: it too had only a policeman's view of government, but it proceeded to apply it to problems that are not susceptible to such treatment. Wilson, at least, knows the limitations of his philosophy.

But once you see the state as a provider of civilizing opportunities, his whole objection collapses. As soon as government begins to supply services, it is turning away from the sterile tyranny of the taboo. The provision of schools, streets, plumbing, highways, libraries, parks, universities, medical attention, post-offices, a Panama Canal, agricultural information, fire protection—is a use of government totally different from the ideal of Jefferson. To furnish these opportunities is to add to the resources of life, and only a doctrinaire adherence to a misunderstood ideal will raise any objection to them.

When an anarchist says that the state must be abolished he does not mean what he says. What he wants to abolish is the repressive, not the productive state. He cannot possibly object to being furnished with the opportunity of writing to his comrade three thousand miles away, of drinking pure water, or taking a walk in the park. Of course when he finds the post-office opening his mail, or a law saying that he must drink nothing but water, he begins to object even to the services of the government. But that is a confusion of thought, for these tyrannies are merely intrusions of the eighteenth century upon the twentieth. The postmaster is still something of a policeman.

Once you realize that moral and social problems must be treated to fine opportunities, that the method of the future is to compete with the devil rather than to curse him; that the furnishing of civilized environments is the goal of statecraft, then there is no longer any reason for keeping social and moral questions out of politics. They are what politics must deal with essentially, now that it has found a way. The policeman with his taboo did make moral and social questions insusceptible to treatment in party platforms. He kept the issues of politics narrow and irrelevant, and just because these really interesting questions could not be handled, politics was an overadvertised hubbub. But the vision of the new statecraft in centering politics upon human interests becomes a creator of opportunities instead of a censor of morals, and deserves a fresh and heightened regard.

The party platform will grow ever more and more into a program of services. In the past it has been an armory of platitudes or a forecast of punishments. It promised that it would stop this evil practice, drive out corruption here, and prosecute this-and-that offense. All that belongs to a moribund tradition. Abuse and disuse characterize the older view of the state: guardian and censor it has been, provider but grudgingly. The proclamations of so-called progressives that they will jail financiers, or "wage relentless warfare" upon social evils, are simply the reiterations of men who do not understand the uses of the state.

A political revolution is in progress: the state as policeman is giving place to the state as producer.

CHAPTER IX

REVOLUTION AND CULTURE

T HERE is a legend of a peasant who lived near Paris through the whole Napoleonic era without ever having heard of the name of Bonaparte. A story of that kind it enough to make a man hesitate before he indulges in a flamboyant description of social changes. That peasant is more than a symbol of the privacy of human interest: he is a warning against the incurable romanticism which clings about the idea of a revolution. Popular history is deceptive if it is used to furnish a picture for coming events. Like drama which compresses the tragedy of a lifetime into a unity of time, place, and action, history foreshortens an epoch into an episode. It gains in poignancy, but loses reality. Men grew from infancy to old age, their children's children had married and loved and worked while the social change we speak of as the industrial revolution was being consummated. That is why it is so difficult for living people to believe that they too art in the midst of great transformations. What looks to us like an incredible rush of events sloping towards a great historical crisis was to our ancestors little else than the occasional punctuation of daily life with an exciting incident. Even to-day when we have begun to speak of our age as a transition, there are millions of people who live in an undisturbed routine. Even those of us who regard ourselves as active in mothering the process and alert in detecting its growth are by no means constantly aware of any great change. For even the fondest mother cannot watch her child grow.

I remember how tremendously surprised I was in visiting Russia several years ago to find that in Moscow or St. Petersburg men were interested in all sorts of things besides the revolution. I had expected every Russian to be absorbed in the struggle. It seemed at first as if my notions of what a revolution ought to be were contradicted everywhere. And I assure you it wrenched the imagination to see tidy nurse-maids wheeling perambulators and children playing diavolo on the very square where Bloody Sunday had gone into history. It takes a long perspective and no very vivid acquaintance with revolution to be melodramatic about it. So much is left out of history and biography which would spoil the effect. The anti-climax is almost always omitted.

Perhaps that is the reason why Arnold Bennett's description of the siege of Paris in "The Old Wives' Tale" is so disconcerting to many people. It is hard to believe that daily life continues with its stretches of boredom and its personal interests even while the enemy is bombarding a city. How much more difficult is it to imagine a revolution that is to come—to space it properly through a long period of time, to conceive what it will be like to the people who live through it. Almost all social prediction is catastrophic and absurdly simplified. Even those who talk of the slow "evolution" of society are likely to think of it as a series of definite changes easily marked and well known to everybody. It is what Bernard Shaw calls the reformer's habit of mistaking his private emotions for a public movement.

Even though the next century is full of dramatic episodes—the collapse of governments and labor wars—these events will be to the social revolution what the smashing of machines in Lancashire was to the industrial revolution. The reality that is worthy of attention is a change in the very texture and quality of millions of lives—a change that will be vividly perceptible only in the retrospect of history.

The conservative often has a sharp sense of the complexity of revolution: not desiring change, he prefers to emphasize its difficulties, whereas the reformer is enticed into a faith that the intensity of desire is a measure of its social effect. Yet just because no reform is in itself a revolution, we must not jump to the assurance that no revolution can be accomplished. True as it is that great changes are imperceptible, it is no less true that they are constantly taking place. Moreover, for the very reason that human life changes its quality so slowly, the panic over political proposals is childish.

It is obvious, for instance, that the recall of judges will not revolutionize the national life. That is why the opposition generated will seem superstitious to the next generation. As I write, a convention of the Populist Party has just taken place. Eight delegates attended the meeting, which was held in a parlor. Even the reactionary press speaks in a kindly way about these men. Twenty years ago the Populists were hated and feared as if they practiced black magic. What they wanted is on the point of realization. To some of us it looks like a drop in the bucket—a slight part of vastly greater plans. But how stupid was the fear of Populism, what unimaginative nonsense it was to suppose twenty years ago that the program was the road to the end of the world.

One good deed or one bad one is no measure of a man's character: the Last Judgment let us hope will be no series of decisions as simple as that. "The soul survives its adventures," says Chesterton with a splendid sense of justice. A country survives its legislation. That truth should not comfort the conservative nor depress the radical. For it means that public policy can enlarge its scope and increase its audacity, can try big experiments without trembling too much over the result. This nation could enter upon the most radical experiments and could afford to fail in them. Mistakes do not affect us so deeply as we imagine. Our prophecies of change are subjective wishes or fears that never come to full realization.

Those socialists are confused who think that a new era can begin by a general strike or an electoral victory. Their critics are just a bit more confused when they become hysterical over the prospect. Both of them over-emphasize the importance of single events. Yet I do not wish to furnish the impression that crises are negligible. They are extremely important as symptoms, as milestones, and as instruments. It is simply that the reality of a revolution is not in a political decree or the scarehead of a newspaper, but in the experiences, feelings, habits of myriad of men.

No one who watched the textile strike at Lawrence, Massachusetts, in the winter of 1912 can forget the astounding effect it had on the complacency of the public.

Very little was revealed that any well-informed social worker does not know as a commonplace about the mill population. The wretchedness and brutality of Lawrence conditions had been described in books and magazines and speeches until radicals had begun to wonder at times whether the power of language wasn't exhausted. The response was discouragingly weak—an occasional government investigation, an impassioned protest from a few individuals, a placid charity, were about all that the middle-class public had to say about factory life. The cynical indifference of legislatures and the hypocrisy of the dominant parties were all that politics had to offer. The Lawrence strike touched the most impervious: story after story came to our ears of hardened reporters who suddenly refused to misrepresent the strikers, of politicians aroused to action, of social workers become revolutionary. Daily conversation was shocked into some contact with realities—the newspapers actually printed facts about the situation of a working class population.

And why? The reason is not far to seek. The Lawrence strikers did something more than insist upon their wrongs; they showed a disposition to right them. That is what scared public opinion into some kind of truth-telling. So long as the poor are docile in their poverty, the rest of us are only too willing to satisfy our consciences by pitying them. But when the down-trodden gather into a threat as they did at Lawrence, when they show that they have no stake in civilization and consequently no respect for its institutions, when the object of pity becomes the avenger of its own miseries, then the middle-class public begins to look at the problem more intelligently.

We are not civilized enough to meet an issue before it becomes acute. We were not intelligent enough to free the slaves peacefully—we are not intelligent enough to-day to meet the industrial problem before it develops a crisis. That is the hard truth of the matter. And that is why no honest student of politics can plead that social movements should confine themselves to argument and debate, abandoning the militancy of the strike, the insurrection, the strategy of social conflict.

Those who deplore the use of force in the labor struggle should ask themselves whether the ruling classes of a country could be depended upon to inaugurate a program of reconstruction which would abolish the barbarism that prevails in industry. Does anyone seriously believe that the business leaders, the makers of opinion and the politicians will, on their own initiative, bring social questions to a solution? If they do it will be for the first time in history. The trivial plans they are introducing to-day—profit-sharing and welfare work—are on their own admission an attempt to quiet the unrest and ward off the menace of socialism.

No, paternalism is not dependable, granting that it is desirable. It will do very little more than it feels compelled to do. Those who to-day bear the brunt of our evils dare not throw themselves upon the mercy of their masters, not though there are bread and circuses as a reward. From the groups upon whom the pressure is most direct must come the power to deal with it. We are not all immediately interested in all problems: our attention wanders unless the people who are interested compel us to listen.

Social movements are at once the symptoms and the

instruments of progress. Ignore them and statesmanship is irrelevant; fail to use them and it is weak. Often in the course of these essays I have quoted from H. G. Wells. I must do so again: "Every party stands essentially for the interests and mental usages of some definite class or group of classes in the exciting community, and every party has its scientific minded and constructive leading section, with well defined hinterlands formulating its social functions in a public spirited form, and its superficial-minded following confessing its meannesses and vanities and prejudices. No class will abolish itself, materially alter its way of living, or drastically reconstruct itself, albeit no class is indisposed to co-operate in the unlimited socialization of any other class. In that capacity for aggression upon other classes lies the essential driving force of modern affairs."

The truth of this can be tested in the socialist movement. There is a section among the socialists which regards the class movement of labor as a driving force in the socialization of industry. This group sees clearly that without the threat of aggression no settlement of the issues is possible. Ordinarily such socialists say that the class struggle is a movement which will end classes. They mean that the self-interest of labor is identical with the interests of a community—that it is a kind of social selfishness. But there are other socialists who speak constantly of "working-class government" and they mean just what they say. It is their intention to have the community ruled in the interests of labor. Probe their minds to find out what they mean by labor and in all honesty you cannot escape the admission that they mean industrial labor alone. These socialists think entirely in terms of the factory population of cities: the farmers, the small shop-keepers, the professional classes have only a perfunctory interest for them. I know that no end of phrases could be adduced to show the inclusiveness of the word labor. But their intention is what I have tried to describe: they are thinking of government by a factory population.

They appeal to history for confirmation: have not all social changes, they ask, meant the emergence of a new economic class until it dominated society? Did not the French Revolution mean the conquest of the feudal landlord by the middle-class merchant? Why should not the Social Revolution mean the victory of the proletariat over the bourgeoisie? That may be true, but it is no reason for being bullied by it into a tame admission that what has always been must always be. I see no reason for exalting the unconscious failures of other revolutions into deliberate models for the next one. Just because the capacity of aggression in the middle class ran away with things, and failed to fuse into any decent social ideal, is not ground for trying as earnestly as possible to repeat the mistake.

The lesson of it all, it seems to me, is this: that class interests are the driving forces which keep public life centered upon essentials. They become dangerous to a nation when it denies them, thwarts them and represses them so long that they burst out and become dominant. Then there is no limit to their aggression until another class appears with contrary interests. The situation might be compared to those hysterias in which a suppressed impulse flares up and rules the whole mental life.

Social life has nothing whatever to fear from group

interests so long as it doesn't try to play the ostrich in regard to them. So the burden of national crises is squarely upon the dominant classes who fight so foolishly against the emergent ones. That is what precipitates violence, that is what renders social co-operation impossible, that is what makes catastrophes the method of change.

The wisest rulers see this. They know that the responsibility for insurrections rests in the last analysis upon the unimaginative greed and endless stupidity of the dominant classes. There is something pathetic in the blindness of powerful people when they face a social crisis. Fighting viciously every readjustment which a nation demands, they make their own overthrow inevitable. It is they who turn opposing interests into a class war. Confronted with the deep insurgency of labor what do capitalists and their spokesmen do? They resist every demand, submit only after a struggle, and prepare a condition of war to the death. When far-sighted men appear in the ruling classes—men who recognize the need of a civilized answer to this increasing restlessness, the rich and the powerful treat them to a scorn and a hatred that are incredibly bitter. The hostility against men like Roosevelt, La Follette, Bryan, Lloyd-George is enough to make an observer believe that the rich of to-day are as stupid as the nobles of France before the Revolution.

It seems to me that Roosevelt never spoke more wisely or as a better friend of civilization than the time when he said at New York City on March 20, 1912, that "the woes of France for a century and a quarter have been due to the folly of her people in splitting into the two camps of unreasonable conservatism and unreasonable radicalism. Had pre-

Revolutionary France listened to men like Turgot and backed them up all would have gone well. But the beneficiaries of privilege, the Bourbon reactionaries, the shortsighted ultra-conservatives, turned down Turgot; and then found that instead of him they had obtained Robespierre. They gained twenty years' freedom from all restraint and reform at the cost of the whirlwind of the red terror; and in their turn the unbridled extremists of the terror induced a blind reaction; and so, with convulsion and oscillation from one extreme to another, with alterations of violent radicalism and violent Bourbonism, the French people went through misery to a shattered goal."

Profound changes are not only necessary, but highly desirable. Even if this country were comfortably well-off, healthy, prosperous, and educated, men would go on inventing and creating opportunities to amplify the possibilities of life. These inventions would mean radical transformations. For we are bent upon establishing more in this nation than a minimum of comfort. A liberal people would welcome social inventions as gladly as we do mechanical ones. What it would fear is a hard-shell resistance to change which brings it about explosively.

Catastrophes are disastrous to radical and conservative alike: they do not preserve what was worth maintaining; they allow a deformed and often monstrous perversion of the original plan. The emancipation of the slaves might teach us the lesson that an explosion followed by reconstruction is satisfactory to nobody.

Statesmanship would go out to meet a crisis before it had become acute. The thing it would emphatically not do is to dam up an insurgent current until it overflowed the countryside. Fight labor's demands to the last ditch and there will come a time when it seizes the whole of power, makes itself sovereign, and takes what it used to ask. That is a poor way for a nation to proceed. For the insurgent become master is a fanatic from the struggle, and as George Santayana says, he is only too likely to redouble his effort after he has forgotten his aim.

Nobody need waste his time debating whether or not there are to be great changes. That is settled for us whether we like it or not. What is worth debating is the method by which change is to come about. Our choice, it seems to me, lies between a blind push and a deliberate leadership, between thwarting movements until they master us, and domesticating them until they are answered.

When Roosevelt formed the Progressive Party on a platform of social reform he crystallized a deep unrest, brought it out of the cellars of resentment into the agora of political discussion. He performed the real task of a leader—a task which has essentially two dimensions. By becoming part of the dynamics of unrest he gathered a power of effectiveness: by formulating a program for insurgency he translated it into terms of public service.

What Roosevelt did at the middle-class level, the socialists have done at the proletarian. The world has been slow to recognize the work of the Socialist Party in transmuting a dumb muttering into a civilized program. It has found an intelligent outlet for forces that would otherwise be purely cataclysmic. The truth of this has been tested recently in the appearance of the "direct actionists."

They are men who have lost faith in political socialism. Why? Because, like all other groups, the socialists tend to become routineers, to slip into an easy reiteration. The direct actionists are a warning to the Socialist Party that its tactics and its program are not adequate to domesticating the deepest unrest of labor. Within that party, therefore, a leadership is required which will ride the forces of "syndicalism" and use them for a constructive purpose. The brilliant writer of the "Notes of the Week" in the English New Age has shown how this might be done. He has fused the insight of the syndicalist with the plans of the collectivists under the name of Guild Socialism.

His plan calls for co-management of industry by the state and the labor union. It steers a course between exploitation by a bureaucracy in the interests of the consumer—the socialist danger—and oppressive monopolies by industrial unions—the syndicalist danger. I shall not attempt to argue here either for or against the scheme. My concern is with method rather than with special pleadings. The Guild Socialism of the "New Age" is merely an instance of statesmanlike dealing with a new social force. Instead of throwing up its hands in horror at one over-advertised tactical incident like sabotage, the "New Age" went straight to the creative impulse of the syndicalist movement.

Every true craftsman, artist or professional man knows and sympathizes with that impulse: you may call it a desire for self-direction in labor. The deepest revolt implied in the term syndicalism is against the impersonal, driven quality of modern industry—against the destruction of that pride which alone distinguishes work from slavery. Some such impulse as that is what marks off syndicalism from the other revolts of labor. Our suspicion of the collectivist arrangement is aroused by the picture of a vast state machine so horribly well-regulated that human impulse is utterly subordinated. I believe too that the fighting qualities of syndicalism are kept at the boiling point by a greater sense of outraged human dignity than can be found among mere socialists or unionists. The imagination is more vivid: the horror of capitalism is not alone in the poverty and suffering it entails, but in its ruthless denial of life to millions of men. The most cruel of all denials is to deprive a human being of joyous activity. Syndicalism is shot through with the assertion that an imposed drudgery is intolerable—that labor at a subsistence wage as a cog in a meaningless machine is no condition upon which to found civilization. That is a new kind of revolt—more dangerous to capitalism than the demand for higher wages. You can not treat the syndicalists like cattle because forsooth they have ceased to be cattle. "The damned wantlessness of the poor," about which Oscar Wilde complained, the cry for a little more fodder, gives way to an insistence upon the chance to be interested in life.

To shut the door in the face of such a current of feeling because it is occasionally exasperated into violence would be as futile as locking up children because they get into mischief. The mind which rejects syndicalism entirely because of the by-products of its despair has had pearls cast before it in vain. I know that syndicalism means a revision of some of our plans—that it is an intrusion upon many a glib prejudice. But a human impulse is more important than any existing theory. We must not throw an unexpected guest out of the window because no place is set for him at table. For we lose not only the charm of his company: he may in anger wreck the house.

Yet the whole nation can't sit at one table: the politician will object that all human interests can't be embodied in a party program. That is true, truer than most politicians would admit in public. No party can represent a whole nation, although, with the exception of the specialists, all of them pretend to do just that. The reason is very simple: a platform is a list of performances that are possible within a few years. It is concerned with more or less immediate proposals, and in a nation split up by class, sectional and racial interests, these proposals are sure to arouse hostility. No definite industrial and political platform, for example, can satisfy rich and poor, black and white, Eastern creditor and Western farmer. A party that tried to answer every conflicting interest would stand still because people were pulling in so many different directions. It would arouse the anger of every group and the approval of its framers. It would have no dynamic power because the forces would neutralize each other.

One comprehensive party platform fusing every interest is impossible and undesirable. What is both possible and desirable is that every group interest should be represented in public life—that it should have spokesmen and influence in public affairs. This is almost impossible to-day. Our blundering political system is pachydermic in its irresponsiveness. The methods of securing representation are unfit instruments for any flexible use. But the United States is evidently not exceptional in this respect. England seems to suffer in the same way. In May, 1912, the "Daily Mail" published a series of articles by H. G. Wells on "The Labour Unrest." Is he not describing almost any session of Congress when he says that "to go into the House of Commons it to go aside out of the general stream of the community's vitality into a corner where little is learnt and much is concocted, into a specialized Assembly which is at once inattentive to and monstrously influential in our affairs?" Further on Wells remarks that "this diminishing actuality of our political life is a matter of almost universal comment to-day. . . . In Great Britain we do not have Elections any more; we have Rejections. What really happens at a general election is that the party organizations—obscure and secretive conclaves with entirely mysterious funds—appoint about 1200 men to be our rulers, and all that we, we so-called self-governing people, are permitted to do is, in a muddled angry way, to strike off the names of about half these selected gentlemen."

A cynic might say that the people can't go far wrong in politics because they can't be very right. Our so-called representative system is unrepresentative in a deeper way than the reformers who talk about the money power imagine. It is empty and thin: a stifling of living currents in the interest of a mediocre regularity.

But suppose that politics were made responsive—suppose that the forces of the community found avenues of expression into public life. Would not our legislatures be cut up into antagonistic parties, would not the conflicts of the nation be concentrated into one heated hail? If you really represented the country in its government, would you not get its partisanship in a quintessential form? After all group interests in the nation are diluted by space and time: the mere separation in cities and country prevents them from falling into the psychology of the crowd. But let them all be represented in one room by men who are professionally interested in their constituency's prejudices and what would you accomplish but a deepening of the cleavages? Would the session not become an interminable wrangle?

Nobody can answer these questions with any certainty. Most prophecies are simply the masquerades of prejudice, and the people who love stability and prefer to let their own well-being alone will see in a sensitive political system little but an invitation to chaos. They will choose facts to adorn their fears. History can be all things to all men: nothing is easier than to summon the Terror, the Commune, lynchings in the Southern States, as witnesses to the excesses and hysterias of the mob. Those facts will prove the case conclusively to anyone who has already made up his mind on the subject. Absolute democrats can also line up their witnesses: the conservatism of the Swiss, Wisconsin's successful experiments, the patience and judgment of the Danes. Both sides are remarkably sure that the right is with them, whereas the only truth about which an observer can be entirely certain is that in some places and in certain instances democracy is admittedly successful.

There is no absolute case one way or the other. It would be silly from the experience we have to make a simple judgment about the value of direct expression. You cannot lump such a mass of events together and come to a single conclusion about them. It is a crude habit of mind that would attempt it. You might as well talk abstractly about the goodness or badness of this universe which contains happiness, pain, exhilaration and indifference in a thousand varying grades and quantities. There is no such thing as Democracy; there are a number of more or less democratic experiments which are not subject to wholesale eulogy or condemnation.

The questions about the success of a truly representative system are pseudo-questions. And for this reason: success is not due to the system; it does not flow from it automatically. The source of success is in the people who use the system: as an instrument it may help or hinder them, but they must operate it. Government is not a machine running on straight tracks to a desired goal. It is a human work which may be facilitated by good tools.

That is why the achievements of the Swiss may mean nothing whatever when you come to prophesy about the people of New York. Because Wisconsin has made good use of the direct primary it does not follow that it will benefit the Filipino. It always seems curious to watch the satisfaction of some reform magazines when China or Turkey or Persia imitates the constitutional forms of Western democracies. Such enthusiasts postulate a uniformity of human ability which every fact of life contradicts.

Present-day reform lays a great emphasis upon instruments and very little on the skilful use of them. It says that human nature is all right, that what is wrong is the "system." Now the effect of this has been to concentrate attention in institutions and to slight men. A small step further, institutions become an end in themselves. They may violate human nature as the taboo does. That does not disturb the interest in them very much, for by common consent reformers are to fix their minds upon the "system."

A machine should be run by men for human uses. The preoccupation with the "system" lays altogether too little stress on the men who operate it and the men for whom it is run. It is as if you put all your effort into the working of a plough and forgot the farmer and the consumer. I state the case baldly and contradiction would be easy. The reformer might point to phrases like "human welfare" which appear in his writings. And yet the point stands, I believe. The emphasis which directs his thinking bears most heavily upon the mechanics of life—only perfunctorily upon the ability of the men who are to use them.

Even an able reformer like Mr. Frederic C. Howe does not escape entirely. A recent book is devoted to a glowing eulogy of "Wisconsin, an Experiment in Democracy:" In a concluding chapter Mr. Howe states the philosophy of the experiment. "What is the explanation of Wisconsin?" he asks. "Why has it been able to eliminate corruption, machine politics, and rid itself of the boss? What is the cause of the efficiency, the thoroughness, the desire to serve which animate the state? Why has Wisconsin succeeded where other states have uniformly failed? I think the explanation is simple. It is also perfectly natural. It is traceable to democracy, to the political freedom which had its beginning in the direct primary law, and which has been continuously strengthened by later laws"; some pages later, "Wisconsin assumed that the trouble with our politics is not with our people, but with the machinery with which the people work. . . . It has established a line of vision as direct as possible between the people and the expression of their will." The impression Mr. Howe evidently wishes to leave with his readers is that the success of the experiment is due to the instruments rather than to the talent of the people of Wisconsin. That would be a valuable and comforting assurance to propagandists, for it means that other states with the same instruments can achieve the same success. But the conclusion seems to me utterly unfounded. The reasoning is perilously like that of the gifted lady amateur who expects to achieve greatness by imitating the paint box and palette, oils and canvases of an artist.

Mr. Howe's own book undermines his conclusions. He begins with an account of La Follette—of a man with initiative and a constructive bent. The forces La Follette set in motion are commented upon. The work of Van Hise is shown. What Wisconsin had was leadership and a people that responded, inventors, and constructive minds. They forged the direct primary and the State University out of the impetus within themselves. No doubt they were fortunate in their choice of instruments. They made the expression of the people's will direct, yet that will surely is the more primary thing. It makes and uses representative systems: but you cannot reverse the process. A man can manufacture a plough and operate it, but no amount of ploughs will create a man and endow him with skill.

All sorts of observers have pointed out that the Western States adopt reform legislation more quickly than the Eastern. Yet no one would seriously maintain that the West is more progressive because it has progressive laws. The laws are a symptom and an aid but certainly not the cause. Constitutions

[*237*]

do not make people; people make constitutions. So the task of reform consists not in presenting a state with progressive laws, but in getting the people to want them.

The practical difference is extraordinary. I insist upon it so much because the tendency of political discussion is to regard government as automatic: a device that is sure to fail or sure to succeed. It is sure of nothing. Effort moves it, intelligence directs it; its fate is in human hands.

The politics I have urged in these chapters cannot be learned by rote. What can be taught by rule of thumb is the administration of precedents. That is at once the easiest and the most fruitless form of public activity. Only a low degree of intelligence is required and of effort merely a persistent repetition. Men fall into a routine when they are tired and slack: it has all the appearance of activity with few of its burdens. It was a profound observation when Bernard Shaw said that men dread liberty because of the bewildering responsibility it imposes and the uncommon alertness it demands. To do what has always been done, to think in well-cut channels, to give up "the intolerable disease of thought," is an almost constant demand of our natures. That is perhaps why so many of the romantic rebels of the Nineteenth Century sank at last into the comforting arms of Mother Church. That is perhaps the reason why most oldish men acquire information, but learn very little. The conservative who loves his routine is in nine cases out of ten a creature too lazy to change its habits.

Confronted with a novelty, the first impulse is to snub it, and send it into exile. When it becomes too persistent to be ignored a taboo is erected and threats of fines and condign punishment are made if it doesn't cease to appear. This is the level of culture at which Sherman Anti-Trust acts are passed, brothels are raided, and labor agitators are thrown into jail. If the taboo is effective it drives the evil under cover, where it festers and emits a slow poison. This is the price we pay for the appearance of suppression. But if the problem is more heavily charged with power, the taboo irritates the force until it explodes. Not infrequently what was once simply a factor of life becomes the dominating part of it. At this point the whole routineer scheme of things collapses, there is a period of convulsion and Cæsarean births, and men weary of excitement sink back into a newer routine. Thus the cycle of futility is completed.

The process bears as much resemblance to statecraft as sitting backward on a runaway horse does to horsemanship. The ordinary politician has no real control, no direction, no insight into the power he rides. What he has is an elevated, though temporary seat. Real statesmanship has a different ambition. It begins by accepting human nature. No routine has ever done that in spite of the conservative patter about "human nature"; mechanical politics has usually begun by ignoring and ended by violating the nature of men.

To accept that nature does not mean that we accept its present character. It is probably true that the impulses of men have changed very little within recorded history. What has changed enormously from epoch to epoch is the character in which these impulses appear. The impulses that at one period work themselves out into cruelty and lust may at another produce the richest values of civilized life. The statesman can affect that choice. His business is to provide fine opportunities for the expression of human impulses—to surround childhood, youth and age with homes and schools, cities and countryside that shall be stocked with interest and the chance for generous activity.

Government can play a leading part in this work, for with the decadence of the church it has become the only truly catholic organization in the land. Its task is essentially to carry out programs of service, to add and build and increase the facilities of life. Repression is an insignificant part of its work; the use of the club can never be applauded, though it may be tolerated *faute de mieux.* Its use is a confession of ignorance.

A sensitively representative machinery will probably serve such statesmanship best. For the easy expression of public opinion in government is a clue to what services are needed and a test of their success. It keeps the processes of politics well ventilated and reminds politicians of their excuse for existence.

In that kind of statesmanship there will be a premium on inventiveness, on the ingenuity to devise and plan. There will be much less use for lawyers and a great deal more for scientists. The work requires industrial organizers, engineers, architects, educators, sanitists to achieve what leadership brings into the program of politics.

This leadership is the distinctive fact about politics. The statesman acts in part as an intermediary between the experts and his constituency. He makes social movements conscious of themselves, expresses their needs, gathers their power and then thrusts them behind the inventor and the technician in the task of actual achievement. What Roosevelt did in the conservation movement was typical of the statesman's work. He recognized the need of attention to natural resources, made it public, crystallized its force and delegated the technical accomplishment to Pinchot and his subordinates.

But creative statesmanship requires a culture to support it. It can neither be taught by rule nor produced out of a vacuum. A community that clatters along with its rusty habits of thought unquestioned, making no distinction between instruments and idols, with a dull consumption of machine-made romantic fiction, no criticism, an empty pulpit and an unreliable press, will find itself faithfully mirrored in public affairs. The one thing that no democrat may assume is that the people are dear good souls, fully competent for their task. The most valuable leaders never assume that. No one, for example, would accuse Karl Marx of disloyalty to workingmen. Yet in 1850 he could write at the demagogues among his friends: "While we draw the attention of the German workman to the *undeveloped state* of the proletariat in Germany, you flatter the national spirit and the guild prejudices of the German artisans in the grossest manner, a method of procedure without doubt the more popular of the two. Just as the democrats made a sort of fetich of the words, 'the people,' so you make one of the word 'proletariat.'" John Spargo quotes this statement in his "Life." Marx, we are told, could use phrases like "democratic miasma." He never seems to have made the mistake of confusing democracy with demolatry. Spargo is perfectly clear about this characteristic of Marx: "He admired most of all, perhaps, that fine devotion to truth as he understood it, and disregard of popularity which marked Owen's life. Contempt for popular opinion was one of his most strongly developed characteristics. He was fond, says Liebknecht, of quoting as his motto the defiat line of Dante, with which he afterwards concluded his preface to 'Das Kapital':

'Segui il tuo corso e lascia dir le genti.'"

It is to Marx's everlasting credit that he set the intellectual standard of socialism on the most vigorous intellectual basis he could find. He knew better than to be satisfied with loose thinking and fairly good intentions. He knew that the vast change he contemplated needed every ounce of intellectual power that the world possessed. A fine boast it was that socialism was equipped with all the culture of the age. I wonder what he would have thought of an enthusiastic socialist candidate for Governor of New York who could write that "until men are free the world has no need of any more literary efforts, of any more paintings, of any more poems. It is better to have said one word for the emancipation of the race than to have written the greatest novel of the times. . . . The world doesn't need any more literature."

I will not venture a guess as to what Marx would have said, but I know what we must say: "Without a literature the people is dumb, without novels and poems, plays and criticism, without books of philosophy, there is neither the intelligence to plan, the imagination to conceive, nor the understanding of a common purpose. Without culture you can knock down governments, overturn property relations, you can create excitement, but you cannot create a genuine revolution in the lives of men." The reply of the workingmen in 1847 to Cabet's proposal that they found Icaria, "a new terrestrial Paradise," in Texas if you please, contains this interesting objection: "Because although those comrades who intend to emigrate with Cabet may be eager Communists, yet they still possess too many of the faults and prejudices of present-day society by reason of their past education to be able to get rid of them at once by joining Icaria."

That simple statement might be taken to heart by all the reformers and socialists who insist that the people are all right, that only institutions are wrong. The politics of reconstruction require a nation vastly better educated, a nation freed from its slovenly ways of thinking, stimulated by wider interests, and jacked up constantly by the sharpest kind of criticism. It is puerile to say that institutions must be changed from top to bottom and then assume that their victims are prepared to make the change. No amount of charters, direct primaries, or short ballots will make a democracy out of an illiterate people. Those portions of America where there are voting booths but no schools cannot possibly be described as democracies. Nor can the person who reads one corrupt newspaper and then goes out to vote make any claim to having registered his will. He may have a will, but he has not used it.

For politics whose only ideal is the routine, it is just as well that men shouldn't know what they want or how to express it. Education has always been a considerable nuisance to the conservative intellect. In the Southern States, culture among the negroes is openly deplored, and I do not blame any patriarch for dreading the education of women.

It is out of culture that the substance of real revolutions is made. If by some magic force you could grant women the vote and then keep them from schools and colleges, newspapers and lectures, the suffrage would be no more effective than a Blue Law against kissing your wife on Sunday. It is democratic machinery with an educated citizenship behind it that embodies all the fears of the conservative and the hopes of the radical.

Culture is the name for what people are interested in, their thoughts, their models, the books they read and the speeches they hear, their tabletalk, gossip, controversies, historical sense and scientific training, the values they appreciate, the quality of life they admire. All communities have a culture. It is the climate of their civilization. Without a favorable culture political schemes are a mere imposition. They will not work without a people to work them.

The real preparation for a creative statesmanship lies deeper than parties and legislatures.

It is the work of publicists and educators, scientists, preachers and artists. Through all the agents that make and popularize thought must come a bent of mind interested in invention and freed from the authority of ideas. The democratic culture must, with critical persistence, make man the measure of all things. I have tried again and again to point out the iconoclasm that is constantly necessary to avoid the distraction that comes of idolizing our own methods of thought. Without an unrelaxing effort to center the mind upon human uses, human purposes, and human results, it drops into idolatry and becomes hostile to creation.

The democratic experiment is the only one that requires

this wilful humanistic culture. An absolutism like Russia's is served better when the people accept their ideas as authoritative and piously sacrifice humanity to a non-human purpose. An aristocracy flourishes where the people find a vicarious enjoyment in admiring the successes of the ruling class. That prevents men from developing their own interests and looking for their own successes. No doubt Napoleon was well content with the philosophy of those guardsmen who drank his health before he executed them.

But those excellent soldiers would make dismal citizens. A view of life in which man obediently allows himself to be made grist for somebody else's mill is the poorest kind of preparation for the work of self-government. You cannot long deny external authorities in government and hold to them for the rest of life, and it is no accident that the nineteenth century questioned a great deal more than the sovereignty of kings. The revolt went deeper and democracy in politics was only an aspect of it. The age might be compared to those years of a boy's life when he becomes an atheist and quarrels with his family. The nineteenth century was a bad time not only for kings, but for priests, the classics, parental autocrats, indissoluble marriage, Shakespeare, the Aristotelian Poetics and the validity of logic. If disobedience is man's original virtue, as Oscar Wilde suggested, it was an extraordinarily virtuous century. Not a little of the revolt was an exuberant rebellion for its own sake. There were also counter-revolutions, deliberate returns to orthodoxy, as in the case of Chesterton. The transvaluation of values was performed by many hands into all sorts of combinations.

There have been other periods of revolution. Heresy is just a few hours younger than orthodoxy. Disobedience is certainly not the discovery of the nineteenth century. But the quality of it is. I believe Chesterton has hold of an essential truth when he says that this is the first time men have boasted of their heresy. The older rebels claimed to be more orthodox than the Church, to have gone back to the true authorities. The radicals of recent times proclaim that there is no orthodoxy, no doctrine that men must accept without question.

Without doubt they deceive themselves mightily. They have their invisible popes, called Art, Nature, Science, with regalia and ritual and a catechism. But they don't mean to have them. They mean to be self-governing in their spiritual lives. And this intention is the half-perceived current which runs through our age and galvanizes so many queer revolts. It would be interesting to trace out the forms it has taken, the abortive cults it has tried and abandoned. In another connection I pointed to autonomy as the hope of syndicalism. It would not be difficult to find a similar assertion in the feminist agitation. From Mrs. Gilman's profound objections against a "man-made" world to the lady who would like to vote about her taxes, there is a feeling that woman must be something more than a passive creature. Walter Pater might be quoted in his conclusion to the effect that "the theory or idea or system which requires of us the sacrifice of any part of experience, in consideration of some interest into which we cannot enter, or some abstract theory we have not identified with ourselves, or what is only conventional, has no real claim upon us." The desire for self-direction has made a thousand philosophies as contradictory as the temperaments of the thinkers. A storehouse of illustration is at hand: Nietzsche advising the creative man to bite off the head of the serpent which is choking him and become "a transfigured being, a light-surrounded being, that *laughed!*" One might point to Stirner's absolute individualism or turn to Whitman's wholehearted acceptance of every man with his catalogue of defects and virtues. Some of these men have cursed each other roundly: Georges Sorel, for example, who urges workingmen to accept none of the bourgeois morality, and becomes most eloquent when he attacks other revolutionists.

I do not wish to suggest too much unanimity in the hundreds of artists and thinkers that are making the thought of our times. There is a kind of "professional reconciler" of opposites who likes to lump all the prominent rebels together and refer to them affectionately as "us radicals." Yet that there is a common impulse in modern thought which strives towards autonomy is true and worth remarking. In some men it is half-conscious, in others a minor influence, but almost no one of weight escapes the contagion of it entirely. It is a new culture that is being prepared. Without it there would to-day be no demand for a creative statesmanship which turns its back upon the routine and the taboo, kings and idols, and non-human purposes. It does more. It is making the atmosphere in which a humanly centered politics can flourish. The fact that this culture is multiform and often contradictory is a sign that more and more of the interests of life are finding expression. We should rejoice at that, for profusion means fertility; where a dead uniformity ceases, invention and ingenuity flourish.

Perhaps the insistence on the need of a culture in state-craft will seem to many people an old fashioned delusion. Among the more rigid socialists and reformers it is not customary to spend much time discussing mental habits. That, they think, was made unnecessary by the discovery of an economic basis of civilization. The destinies of society are felt to be too solidly set in industrial conditions to allow any cultural direction. Where there is no choice, of what importance is opinion?

All propaganda is, of course, a practical tribute to the value of culture. However inevitable the process may seem, all socialists agree that its inevitability should be fully realized. They teach at one time that men act from class interests: but they devote an enormous amount of energy to making men conscious of their class. It evidently matters to that supposedly inevitable progress whether men are aware of it. In short, the most hardened socialist admits choice and deliberation, culture and ideals into his working faith. He may talk as if there were an iron determinism, but his practice is better than his preachment.

Yet there are necessities in social life. To all the purposes of politics it is settled, for instance, that the trust will never be "unscrambled" into small competing businesses. We say in our argument that a return to the days of the stage-coach is impossible or that "you cannot turn back the hands of the clock." Now man might return to the stage-coach if that seemed to him the supreme goal of all his effort, just as anyone can follow Chesterton's advice to turn back the hands of the clock if be pleases. But nobody can recover his yesterdays no matter how much he abuses the clock, and no man can expunge the memory of railroads though all the stations and engines were dismantled.

"From this survival of the past," says Bergson, "it follows that consciousness cannot go through the same state twice." This is the real necessity that makes any return to the imagined glories of other days an idle dream. Graham Wallas remarks that those who have eaten of the tree of knowledge cannot forget—"Mr. Chesterton cries out, like the Cyclops in the play, against those who complicate the life of man, and tells us to eat 'caviare on impulse,' instead of 'grapenuts on principle.' But since we cannot unlearn our knowledge, Mr. Chesterton is only telling us to eat caviare on principle." The binding fact we must face in all our calculations, and so in politics too, is that you cannot recover what is passed. That is why educated people are not to be pressed into the customs of their ignorance, why women who have reached out for more than "Kirche, Kinder und Küche" can never again be entirely domestic and private in their lives. Once people have questioned an authority their faith has lost its naïveté. Once men have tasted inventions like the trust they have learned something which cannot be annihilated. I know of one reformer who devotes a good deal of his time to intimate talks with powerful conservatives. He explains them to themselves: never after do they exercise their power with the same unquestioning ruthlessness.

Life is an irreversible process and for that reason its future can never be a repetition of the past. This insight we owe to Bergson. The application of it to politics is not difficult because politics is one of the interests of life. We can learn from him in what sense we are bound. "The finished portrait is explained by the features of the model, by the nature of the artist, by colors spread out on the palette; but even with the knowledge of what explains it, no one, not even the artist, could have foreseen exactly what the portrait would be, for to predict it would have been to produce it before it was produced. . . ." The future is explained by the economic and social institutions which were present at its birth: the trust and the labor union, all the "movements" and institutions, will condition it. "Just as the talent of the painter is formed or deformed—in any case, is modified—under the very influence of the work he produces, so each of our states, at the moment of its issue, modifies our personality, being indeed the new form we are just assuming. It is then right to say that what we do depends on what we are; but it is necessary to add also, that we are, to a certain extent, what we do, and that we are creating ourselves continually."

What I have called culture enters into political life as a very powerful condition. It is a way of creating ourselves. Make a blind struggle luminous, drag an unconscious impulse into the open day, see that men are aware of their necessities, and the future is in a measure controlled. The culture of to-day is for the future an historical condition. That is its political importance. The mental habits we are forming, our philosophies and magazines, theaters, debates, schools, pulpits and newspapers become part of an active past which as Bergson says "follows us at every instant; all that we have felt, thought, and willed from our earliest infancy is there, leaning over the present which is about to join it, pressing against the portals of consciousness that would fain leave it outside."

Revolution and Culture

Socialists claim that because the McNamara brothers had no "class-consciousness," because they were without a philosophy of society and an understanding of the labor movement their sense of wrong was bound to seek out dynamite. That is a profound truth backed by abundant evidence. If you turn, for example, to Spargo's Life of Karl Marx you see that all through his career Marx struggled with the mere insurrectionists. It was the men without the Marxian vision of growth and discipline who were forever trying to lead little marauding bands against the governments of Europe. The fact is worth pondering: the Marxian socialists, openly declaring that all authority is a temporary manifestation of social conditions, have waged what we must call a war of culture against the powers of the world. They have tried to arouse in workingmen the consciousness of an historical mission—the patience of that labor is one of the wonders of the age. But the McNamaras had a culture that could help them not at all. They were Catholics, Democrats and old-fashioned trade-unionists. Religion told them that authority was absolute and eternal, politics that Jefferson had said about all there was to say, economics insisted that the struggle between labor and capital was an everlasting see-saw. But life told them that society was brutal: an episode like the shirtwaist factory fire drove them to blasphemy and dynamite.

Those bombs at Los Angeles, assassination and terrorism, are compounded of courage, indignation and ignorance. Civilization has much to fear from the blind class antagonisms it fosters; but the preaching of "class consciousness," far from being a fomenter of violence, must be recognized as the civilizing influence of culture upon economic interests.

Thoughts and feelings count. We live in a revolutionary period and nothing is so important as to be aware of it. The measure of our self-consciousness will more or less determine whether we are to be the victims or the masters of change. Without philosophy we stumble along. The old routines and the old taboos are breaking up anyway, social forces are emerging which seek autonomy and struggle against slavery to non-human purposes. We seem to be moving towards some such statecraft as I have tried to suggest. But without knowledge of it that progress will be checkered and perhaps futile. The dynamics for a splendid human civilization are all about us. They need to be used. For that there must be a culture practiced in seeking the inwardness of impulses, competent to ward off the idols of its own thought, hospitable to novelty and sufficiently inventive to harness power.

Why this age should have come to be what it is, why at this particular time the whole drift of thought should be from authority to autonomy would be an interesting speculation. It is one of the ultimate questions of politics. It is like asking why Athens in the Fifth Century B. C. was singled out as the luminous point of the Western World. We do not know enough to cut under such mysteries. We can only begin to guess why there was a Renaissance, why in certain centuries man seems extraordinarily creative. Perhaps the Modern Period with its flexibility, sense of change, and desire for self-direction is a liberation due to the great surplus of wealth. Perhaps the ease of travel, the popularizing of knowledge, the break-down of frontiers have given us a new interest in human life by showing how temporary are all its instruments. Certainly placid or morose acceptance is undermined. If men remain slaves either to ideas or to other men, it will be because they do not know they are slaves. Their intention is to be free. Their desire is for a full and expressive life and they do not relish a lop-sided and lamed humanity. For the age is rich with varied and generous passions.

GREAT MINDS PAPERBACK SERIES

ART

❏ Leonardo da Vinci—*A Treatise on Painting*

CRITICAL ESSAYS

❏ Desiderius Erasmus—*The Praise of Folly*
❏ Jonathan Swift—*A Modest Proposal and Other Satires*
❏ H. G. Wells—*The Conquest of Time*

ECONOMICS

❏ Charlotte Perkins Gilman—*Women and Economics:*
      A Study of the Economic Relation between Women and Men
❏ John Maynard Keynes—*The End of Laissez-Faire* and
      The Economic Consequences of the Peace
❏ John Maynard Keynes—*The General Theory of Employment, Interest, and Money*
❏ John Maynard Keynes—*A Tract on Monetary Reform*
❏ Thomas R. Malthus—*An Essay on the Principle of Population*
❏ Alfred Marshall—*Money, Credit, and Commerce*
❏ Alfred Marshall—*Principles of Economics*
❏ Karl Marx—*Theories of Surplus Value*
❏ John Stuart Mill—*Principles of Political Economy*
❏ David Ricardo—*Principles of Political Economy and Taxation*
❏ Adam Smith—*Wealth of Nations*
❏ Thorstein Veblen—*Theory of the Leisure Class*

HISTORY

❏ Edward Gibbon—*On Christianity*
❏ Alexander Hamilton, John Jay, and James Madison—*The Federalist*
❏ Herodotus—*The History*
❏ Thucydides—*History of the Peloponnesian War*
❏ Andrew D. White—*A History of the Warfare of Science with Theology*
      in Christendom

LAW

❏ John Austin—*The Province of Jurisprudence Determined*

POLITICS

❏ Walter Lippmann—*A Preface to Politics*

PSYCHOLOGY

❏ Sigmund Freud—*Totem and Taboo*

RELIGION

❏ Thomas Henry Huxley—*Agnosticism and Christianity and Other Essays*
❏ Ernest Renan—*The Life of Jesus*
❏ Upton Sinclair—*The Profits of Religion*
❏ Elizabeth Cady Stanton—*The Woman's Bible*
❏ Voltaire—*A Treatise on Toleration and Other Essays*

SCIENCE

- ❏ Jacob Bronowski—*The Identity of Man*
- ❏ Nicolaus Copernicus—*On the Revolutions of Heavenly Spheres*
- ❏ Francis Crick—*Of Molecules and Men*
- ❏ Marie Curie—*Radioactive Substances*
- ❏ Charles Darwin—*The Autobiography of Charles Darwin*
- ❏ Charles Darwin—*The Descent of Man*
- ❏ Charles Darwin—*The Origin of Species*
- ❏ Charles Darwin—*The Voyage of the* Beagle
- ❏ René Descartes—*Treatise of Man*
- ❏ Albert Einstein—*Relativity*
- ❏ Michael Faraday—*The Forces of Matter*
- ❏ Galileo Galilei—*Dialogues Concerning Two New Sciences*
- ❏ Ernst Haeckel—*The Riddle of the Universe*
- ❏ William Harvey—*On the Motion of the Heart and Blood in Animals*
- ❏ Werner Heisenberg—*Physics and Philosophy: The Revolution in Modern Science*
- ❏ Fred Hoyle—*Of Men and Galaxies*
- ❏ Julian Huxley—*Evolutionary Humanism*
- ❏ Thomas H. Huxley—*Evolution and Ethics* and *Science and Morals*
- ❏ Edward Jenner—*Vaccination against Smallpox*
- ❏ Johannes Kepler—*Epitome of Copernican Astronomy* and *Harmonies of the World*
- ❏ Charles Mackay—*Extraordinary Popular Delusions and the Madness of Crowds*
- ❏ James Clerk Maxwell—*Matter and Motion*
- ❏ Isaac Newton—*Opticks, Or Treatise of the Reflections, Inflections, and Colours of Light*
- ❏ Isaac Newton—*The Principia*
- ❏ Louis Pasteur and Joseph Lister—*Germ Theory and Its Application to Medicine* and *On the Antiseptic Principle of the Practice of Surgery*
- ❏ William Thomson (Lord Kelvin) and Peter Guthrie Tait—*The Elements of Natural Philosophy*
- ❏ Alfred Russel Wallace—*Island Life*

SOCIOLOGY

- ❏ Emile Durkheim—*Ethics and the Sociology of Morals*

GREAT BOOKS IN PHILOSOPHY PAPERBACK SERIES

ESTHETICS

- ❏ Aristotle—*The Poetics*
- ❏ Aristotle—*Treatise on Rhetoric*

ETHICS

- ❏ Aristotle—*The Nicomachean Ethics*
- ❏ Marcus Aurelius—*Meditations*
- ❏ Jeremy Bentham—*The Principles of Morals and Legislation*
- ❏ John Dewey—*Human Nature and Conduct*
- ❏ John Dewey—*The Moral Writings of John Dewey, Revised Edition*
- ❏ Epictetus—*Enchiridion*
- ❏ David Hume—*An Enquiry Concerning the Principles of Morals*
- ❏ Immanuel Kant—*Fundamental Principles of the Metaphysic of Morals*
- ❏ John Stuart Mill—*Utilitarianism*
- ❏ George Edward Moore—*Principia Ethica*
- ❏ Friedrich Nietzsche—*Beyond Good and Evil*

- ❏ Plato—*Protagoras, Philebus*, and *Gorgias*
- ❏ Bertrand Russell—*Bertrand Russell On Ethics, Sex, and Marriage*
- ❏ Arthur Schopenhauer—*The Wisdom of Life* and *Counsels and Maxims*
- ❏ Adam Smith—*The Theory of Moral Sentiments*
- ❏ Benedict de Spinoza—*Ethics* and *The Improvement of the Understanding*

LOGIC

- ❏ George Boole—*The Laws of Thought*

METAPHYSICS/EPISTEMOLOGY

- ❏ Aristotle—*De Anima*
- ❏ Aristotle—*The Metaphysics*
- ❏ Francis Bacon—*Essays*
- ❏ George Berkeley—*Three Dialogues Between Hylas and Philonous*
- ❏ W. K. Clifford—*The Ethics of Belief and Other Essays*
- ❏ René Descartes—*Discourse on Method* and *The Meditations*
- ❏ John Dewey—*How We Think*
- ❏ John Dewey—*The Influence of Darwin on Philosophy and Other Essays*
- ❏ Epicurus—*The Essential Epicurus: Letters, Principal Doctrines, Vatican Sayings, and Fragments*
- ❏ Sidney Hook—*The Quest for Being*
- ❏ David Hume—*An Enquiry Concerning Human Understanding*
- ❏ David Hume—*Treatise of Human Nature*
- ❏ William James—*The Meaning of Truth*
- ❏ William James—*Pragmatism*
- ❏ Immanuel Kant—*The Critique of Judgment*
- ❏ Immanuel Kant—*Critique of Practical Reason*
- ❏ Immanuel Kant—*Critique of Pure Reason*
- ❏ Gottfried Wilhelm Leibniz—*Discourse on Metaphysics* and the *Monadology*
- ❏ John Locke—*An Essay Concerning Human Understanding*
- ❏ George Herbert Mead—*The Philosophy of the Present*
- ❏ Michel de Montaigne—*Essays*
- ❏ Charles S. Peirce—*The Essential Writings*
- ❏ Plato—*The Euthyphro, Apology, Crito*, and *Phaedo*
- ❏ Plato—*Lysis, Phaedrus*, and *Symposium*
- ❏ Bertrand Russell—*The Problems of Philosophy*
- ❏ George Santayana—*The Life of Reason*
- ❏ Sextus Empiricus—*Outlines of Pyrrhonism*
- ❏ Ludwig Wittgenstein—*Wittgenstein's Lectures: Cambridge, 1932–1935*
- ❏ Alfred North Whitehead—*The Concept of Nature*

PHILOSOPHY OF RELIGION

- ❏ Jeremy Bentham—*The Influence of Natural Religion on the Temporal Happiness of Mankind*
- ❏ Marcus Tullius Cicero—*The Nature of the Gods* and *On Divination*
- ❏ Ludwig Feuerbach—*The Essence of Christianity* and *The Essence of Religion*
- ❏ Paul Henry Thiry, Baron d'Holbach—*Good Sense*
- ❏ David Hume—*Dialogues Concerning Natural Religion*
- ❏ William James—*The Varieties of Religious Experience*
- ❏ John Locke—*A Letter Concerning Toleration*
- ❏ Lucretius—*On the Nature of Things*
- ❏ John Stuart Mill—*Three Essays on Religion*
- ❏ Friedrich Nietzsche—*The Antichrist*

☐ Thomas Paine—*The Age of Reason*
☐ Bertrand Russell—*Bertrand Russell On God and Religion*

SOCIAL AND POLITICAL PHILOSOPHY

☐ Aristotle—*The Politics*
☐ Mikhail Bakunin—*The Basic Bakunin: Writings, 1869–1871*
☐ Edmund Burke—*Reflections on the Revolution in France*
☐ John Dewey—*Freedom and Culture*
☐ John Dewey—*Individualism Old and New*
☐ John Dewey—*Liberalism and Social Action*
☐ G. W. F. Hegel—*The Philosophy of History*
☐ G. W. F. Hegel—*Philosophy of Right*
☐ Thomas Hobbes—*The Leviathan*
☐ Sidney Hook—*Paradoxes of Freedom*
☐ Sidney Hook—*Reason, Social Myths, and Democracy*
☐ John Locke—*Second Treatise on Civil Government*
☐ Niccolo Machiavelli—*The Prince*
☐ Karl Marx (with Friedrich Engels)—*The German Ideology,* including
   Theses on Feuerbach and Introduction to the Critique of Political Economy
☐ Karl Marx—*The Poverty of Philosophy*
☐ Karl Marx/Friedrich Engels—*The Economic and Philosophic Manuscripts of 1844*
   and *The Communist Manifesto*
☐ John Stuart Mill—*Considerations on Representative Government*
☐ John Stuart Mill—*On Liberty*
☐ John Stuart Mill—*On Socialism*
☐ John Stuart Mill—*The Subjection of Women*
☐ Montesquieu, Charles de Secondat—*The Spirit of Laws*
☐ Friedrich Nietzsche—*Thus Spake Zarathustra*
☐ Thomas Paine—*Common Sense*
☐ Thomas Paine—*Rights of Man*
☐ Plato—*Laws*
☐ Plato—*The Republic*
☐ Jean-Jacques Rousseau—*Émile*
☐ Jean-Jacques Rousseau—*The Social Contract*
☐ Bertrand Russell—*Political Ideas*
☐ Mary Wollstonecraft—*A Vindication of the Rights of Men*
☐ Mary Wollstonecraft—*A Vindication of the Rights of Women*